Opening a Door

Reading Poetry in the Middle School Classroom

by Paul B. Janeczko

"Not knowing when the dawn will come, I open every door."
—Emily Dickinson

SCHOLASTIC
PROFESSIONAL BOOKS

NEW YORK · TORONTO · LONDON · AUCKLAND · SYDNEY
MEXICO CITY · NEW DELHI · HONG KONG

Cover design and illustration by James Sarfati
Interior design by LDL Designs

ISBN 0-439-33207-9
Copyright © 2003 by Paul B. Janeczko
All rights reserved.
Printed in the U.S.A.
1 2 3 4 5 6 7 8 9 10   23   09 08 07 06 05 04 03

Table of Contents

Dedication

for Jim Pierce

an old friend
and
a man of honor

Acknowledgements

Few writers are blessed with two thoughtful and astute editors on a single book. I am one of the lucky ones. Wendy Murray helped me get the project off the ground, kicking me in the pants when I needed it, patting me on the back when I deserved it. When Wendy left the project to bring a gorgeous daughter into the world, Ray Coutu took over before panic set in. He was there when I needed him, offering advice and encouragement, not to mention his editorial savvy. I am grateful for their help. This book would have been less without it.

Foreword

Poetry is something to enjoy. To many of us, that may sound like an obvious truth. But to others, both teachers and students, poetry is a kind of sulfur-and-molasses tonic to be choked down only because it's good for you.

Teachers who regard poetry as enjoyable are the lucky ones. For them, teaching it is usually an agreeable task. Those of the opposite opinion need not feel ashamed. They are probably suffering from miserable experiences, encounters with dull or uncongenial poems, which they had to analyze in college courses. In this book, teachers of either persuasion will find a valuable ally.

For a long time, Paul B. Janeczko has devoted his energies to combating grim assumptions about poetry. When he began teaching in high school, he had to cast aside certain notions, such as the one that there's nothing to be done with a poem but analyze it. In the first part of *Opening a Door,* he confides that he once found poetry hard to put across to students, but when he brought in poems that spoke directly to them, his classes improved mightily.

Janeczko, you see, speaks of hard-won experience. Besides spending many years as a high school teacher, he has worked as a visiting poet in middle and elementary schools, encouraging kids to read poems and write poems of their own. He is familiar with the frontline warfare in which most middle school teachers are engaged—the endless struggle against student indifference. It helps that he himself is a poet of considerable accomplishment (see his collection for young people, *Brickyard Summer*), and one of the nation's finest and hardest-working anthologists. Single-handedly, he has been a driving force in advancing wider acceptance of poetry in school curricula.

I first met Janeczko's work in 1977, in *The Crystal Image,* a popular paperback anthology of poems. He seemed to me then, as he seems still, a sensitive chooser of poetry for children and young people, unusual in the depth and breadth of his taste. Since then, Janeczko has edited a host of esteemed anthologies. A Janeczko anthology is always rife with discoveries. Unwilling to do as some anthologists do, merely lift the discoveries of other anthologists, he apparently reads, chews, and digests stacks of current poetry, then thinks and feels for himself. At the same time, Janeczko is well grounded in the poetry of the past. His love of poetry shows, but he is quick to admit that students aren't necessarily going to like every poem he loves.

Whether a poem is new or old, he believes, doesn't matter to students: "It need only be poetry that is accessible to them." And he adds, "which doesn't mean it must be simple and shallow. I want

> "This engaging book… suggests ways to encourage your students to venture deeply into a poem—not just shrug and say, 'I love it' or 'I hate it.' It questions students' assumption that a poem is written in a kind of secret code to which only the teacher has the key."

my students to stretch their intellects when they read a poem, to let their hearts grow." Clearly, we're in the presence of a wise and compassionate teacher who knows that poems aren't easily graspable, yet is determined to help students obtain the highest possible reward.

With *Opening a Door,* Janeczko has made a fresh and serious contribution to the literature on teaching poetry. This engaging book won't take long to read, but it delivers a kit of valuable instruments. It suggests ways to encourage your students to venture deeply into a poem—not just shrug and say, "I love it" or "I hate it." It questions students' assumption that a poem is written in a kind of secret code to which only the teacher has the key. His "Explorations"—as he calls his classroom-tested strategies—aren't maps of highways you have to stick to. They lead you to byways, upon which you are free to wander and make personal discoveries along the way.

Middle school students often arrive at the classroom suffering from the assumption that they've seen everything, know everything, and don't need to be told. Paul B. Janeczko is tuned to their wavelength, as you can see from his discussion of William Stafford's "Fifteen" on page 11. This poem, he says, explores the "angst" of being an adolescent. Browse *Opening a Door* and you'll find many more insights into your students' world.

If by using some of the strategies Janeczko sets forth you can lighten your task, find more satisfaction in your work, and help nurture in your students an expandable love for poetry, then this book will be worth its weight in gold. I'd give it a try.

—X. J. Kennedy

PART 1:
Becoming a Teacher of Poetry

"Ode to Melancholy," by John Keats, is the first poem I remember teaching during my rookie year in the high school classroom. To prepare for the lesson, I spent a good part of the weekend before doing what I had been taught in my methods classes and what my professors had modeled for me in grad school. I checked every single explanatory footnote on the poem in my weighty Norton's anthology. I read a stack of dim photo-copied articles from scholarly journals that placed the poem in the tradition of Romantic poets. I brushed up on Keats' sadly short life, from his birth above his father's livery stable to his death from tuberculosis 25 years later. I even wrote out on file cards the series of "Helpful Questions" from the teacher's guide to the literature text the class was using. I was ready to teach a poem!

Luckily, my students were kind to me that day. I began class with my brief lecture on Keats, aug-menting the information given in our text. Sure, I noticed the disguised yawns, the polite glances at the wall clock, but I was teaching poetry. The clock be damned! Then I read the poem aloud as the students followed along in the book. When I looked up, I saw that no one seemed moved by the poem. I asked a boy to read the poem aloud. He stumbled and bumbled his way through it, befud-dled by its vocabulary and syntax, not to mention its subject matter. "Any questions?" I asked. None. In the silence I could almost hear Keats weeping for his poem.

I quickly began to plow through my helpful question cards. With some prompting—okay, with some serious prompting—my students were able to answer most of the questions. Those they couldn't answer, I answered for them. A few students took notes. Some glanced at the clock. Two or three, girls naturally, actually seemed inter-ested in this poem written nearly 150 years earlier. But the truth was that most of these tenth graders from a middle-class Cleveland suburb didn't know what to make of the poem's "rosary of yew-berries," its "rainbow of the

> "I asked a boy to read the poem aloud. He stumbled and bumbled his way through it... 'Any questions?' I asked. None. In the silence, I could almost hear Keats weeping for his poem."

salt sand-wave," or its "mournful Psyche."

It was my turn to look at the clock. I thought for sure the period was about to end. Not so. Only half of it had ached by. I looked at the kids. They looked at me. "Any questions?" I asked. There was just one: "Are we finished with this poem?" I nodded—and heard a dozen books softly thump closed—then mumbled that they should use the remaining time to study.

By the time I mustered the courage to present poetry to the class again, I had learned one lesson from that initial debacle: Never bring only one poem to class. So, for the next lesson, I brought in three poems, for which I had dutifully prepared a biographical lecture, pertinent footnote fodder—the sort of stuff Coleman Barks, poet and Rumi translator, called "chew-toys for the intellect" (Barks, 1995)—and more "discussion" questions. And, unlike the previous class, I managed to fill the entire period. At the time, I thought that was a good thing, not realizing that I had only managed to double our agony.

After half a dozen such numbing poetry classes, I reluctantly brought up my problem at a department meeting. I say "reluctantly" because I was "the kid" and didn't want the veterans to know of my failures.

"I don't get it," I moaned. "I spent so much time preparing the lessons."

"Don't feel bad," Roger, a ten-year teacher, told me. "Kids just don't like poetry. They don't get it. Period."

I sat in my silence as other members of the department added their two cents. With one exception—the department head who assured me that his advanced English students "got" every poem he taught—my fellow teachers had resigned themselves to the fact that kids just don't like poetry. What else could it be? We were, after all, teaching them some of the greatest poetry of all time.

As the discussion continued, I began to realize that most of my colleagues had simply given up on poetry. They entered the classroom with good intentions: to teach the classic poems of the English language the way they had been taught—to explicate and analyze each line of every poem. But they soon saw that such an approach didn't engage their students, so they taught less poetry the following year. Slowly but surely, they were being pulled down a spiral that continued until they reached bottom and "did" only enough poetry to satisfy the curriculum requirements.

> "My fellow teachers had resigned themselves to the fact that kids just don't like poetry. What else could it be? We were, after all, teaching them some of the greatest poetry of all time."

But I loved poetry. I agreed with James Dickey, who said in an interview: "What you have to realize…is that poetry is just naturally the greatest goddamn thing that ever was in the whole universe. If you love it, there's no substitute for it" (Packard, 1974). As an undergrad, I had started reading a lot of poetry. Some was for class assignments—assignments that inspired me to do more poetry reading on my own. I wish I could name the poet who transformed me from a non-poetry-reading high school student to a college-level devotee, but I can't. It may have been William Butler Yeats, who touched me with "When You Are Old," his poem of long-lasting love. Or, maybe it was Walt Whitman, the Good Gray Poet, whose robust voice resonated in his long, sprawling lines. Or, it could have been Emily Dickinson, who noted with remarkable clarity in her short, precise poems the details of the world around her Amherst, Massachusetts, home. Most likely it was the poetry itself that showed me what poetry could be.

The more poetry I read, the more good poems I discovered. I became a poetry junkie. I read poetry the way some people watch soap operas, work their gardens, or follow the Red Sox: irrationally, compulsively, endlessly. I read poems nearly every day whenever I found myself with a few unfilled minutes. Why couldn't I instill in my students this passion for poetry?

After all of my colleagues had gone home for the day, I realized that I wasn't surprised by what they had told me in the meeting. After all, we were only doing what we had learned in our training. For me that education came in graduate school. While the university was rightfully preparing my classmates and me to be scholars, or at least to be scholarly, I was uneasy about how I would take what I had learned in my classes and make it "relevant" (that was the buzz word of the day) for my students. My graduate study seemed designed to create a distance between the poem and the reader. And I knew that the poems that meant the most to me were poems that invited me closer, to feel, in a sense, the very heartbeat of the poem. I didn't want to approach it with the detachment of a coroner examining a corpse.

> "The more poetry I read, the more good poems I discovered. I became a poetry junkie. I read poetry the way some people watch soap operas, work their gardens, or follow the Red Sox: irrationally, compulsively, endlessly."

Reading a poem should not be like performing an autopsy, looking at a dead object and figuring out what killed it. Or, worse, trying to figure out what it might have been like when it was alive. Good poems are alive, as alive as a cat sunning itself on a warm windowsill, a power hitter

> "Reading a poem should not be like performing an autopsy, looking at a dead object and figuring out what killed it. Or, worse, trying to figure out what it might have been like when it was alive. Good poems *are* alive..."

driving a hanging curve ball deep into the bleachers, or Van Gogh's "Irises" hanging on the wall of a big city museum. We can enjoy and examine these things without taking away their life, their mystery. No wonder Molly Peacock admired one of her literature professors who had "the sense to leave poems whole even as he investigated them" (Peacock, 1999).

Throwing Out the Book on What We've Learned About Teaching Poetry

As I considered how to change my approach, I realized that if I was going to make poetry important for my students—I was even hopeful that a few might find poetry as exciting as I did—I was going to have to learn to do it on my own. Why not take some of those poems that I loved so much and try them out with my students? I wouldn't have the canned questions from the teacher's guide to rely on. But, truth be told, they hadn't served me well anyway. I left school that afternoon determined to draw up a new lesson that would, in a sense, throw out the book on what I had learned about teaching poetry.

Rather than rely on our literature textbook, I turned to my own favorite poetry anthologies, grabbing first *Reflections on a Gift of Watermelon Pickle* (edited by Stephen Dunning, Edward Lueders, and Hugh Smith), an anthology that was truly a groundbreaking collection. Not only did it contain outstanding contemporary poetry, but it interspersed black-and-white photographs as counterpoints to the poems. As I paged through it, I immediately found several poems that I felt certain would work with my students, poems that reflected what Ted Hughes had written in *Poetry Is:* "Poetry is not made out of thoughts and casual fancies. It is made out of experiences which change our bodies, and spirits, whether momentarily or for good" (Hughes, 1970).

I found poems that, I thought, told of such experiences: "Too Blue" by Langston Hughes, with a speaker who has "got those sad old weary blues;" "Loneliness" by Brooks Jenkins, with a narrator who takes the time to listen to an old man; and "Fifteen" by William Stafford. I was especially exciting about sharing the Stafford poem with my students:

South of the bridge on Seventeenth
I found back of the willows one summer
day a motorcycle with engine running
as it lay on its side, ticking over
slowly in the high grass. I was fifteen.

I admired all that pulsing gleam, the
shiny flanks, the demure headlights
fringed where it lay; I led it gently
to the road and stood with that
companion, ready and friendly. I was fifteen.

We could find the end of a road, meet
the sky on out Seventeenth. I thought about
hills, and patting the handle got back a
confident opinion. On the bridge we indulged
a forward feeling, a tremble. I was fifteen.

Thinking, back farther in the grass I found
the owner, just coming to, where he had flipped
over the rail. He had blood on his hand, was pale—
I helped him walk to his machine. He ran his hand
over it, called me a good man, roared away.

I stood there, fifteen.

Stafford's poem explores much of the angst of being a fifteen-year-old boy. The narrator is captivated by a motorcycle lying in the high grass, with its "pulsing gleam, the/shiny flanks, the demure headlights." He treats it like an injured animal, leading it "gently" to the road, where it became his "companion, ready and friendly." Ready for what? To take off! In the next stanza the boy and the motorcycle become one: "We could find the end of a road, meet/the sky." The open road calls this kid. He thinks "about/hills." He pats the handlebars and gets back a "confident opinion." He is ready to roll: "On the bridge we indulged/a forward feeling, a tremble." But, of course, he doesn't ride away but, rather, he is left with the hollow satisfaction of having the owner of the bike call him "good man" before he "roared away."

Stafford tells the boy's story in four stanzas. The first three end with a refrain, a lament almost: "I was fifteen." That fact is inescapable for the boy. He begins the poem alone, then is part of "We" as he bonds with the bike. At the end of the poem, his reality returns: "I stood there, fifteen." And what about that end of the poem? Would it surprise my students when they read it? That would be a question I would pursue with them. I prepared other questions, too:

- What's it like to be 15?
- What's the best thing about being 15?
- What's the worst thing about that age?
- What do you think this kid's life is like?
- Have you ever thought of just taking off?
- Where would go? What would you do?

My students could talk as well about the elements of the poem: Stafford's use of the refrain "I was fifteen," his conversational tone, and his word choice. I would ask them to consider other aspects of the poem. I would ask them to examine the details that Stafford used to describe the motorcycle, especially in the first and second stanzas. What details does he use? I'd ask my students to consider why Stafford spends only two lines in the last stanza to show the rider walking to his motorcycle and taking off.

I prepped the Stafford poem and two others. This time the questions on my file cards were of my creation, based on my reading of the poems, and what I perceived to be my students' interest in the issues that the poems presented. When I walked into that classroom the next day, I was ready to present poetry that spoke to my kids.

The rest, as they say, is history. I'd like to report that, by the end of class, the students were pounding on the desks demanding more poetry. Not so. But I did consider the class a success. The poems held their attention. I did get the students to discuss the poems—truly discuss them, not simply give vague answers to my erudite questions.

But the revelations of that class went far beyond that day. Well beyond that year, in fact. That class sent me in a direction that I have followed throughout my teaching career. Since that day, over 30 years ago, one belief has been my North Star: Students will read and discuss carefully selected poetry. It doesn't have to be contemporary poetry. It need only be poetry that is accessible to them, which doesn't mean it must be simple and shallow. I want my students to stretch their intellects when they read a poem, to let their hearts grow. But, at the same time, I want them to have every chance to succeed when they reach. They don't have to like every poem I select—and they certainly haven't—but I ask them to give each poem a fair chance to touch them. In other words, I want students to be more directly involved with poetry. And my job is to find quality poems that allow for that to happen.

> "[Students] don't have to like every poem I select— and they certainly haven't—but I ask them to give each poem a fair chance to touch them."

Choosing Poems Carefully

Before we can expect our students to explore poems we need to make sure we select with care the poems we share with them. The poems should allow the students the opportunity to make personal connections, although the poems need not exactly mirror their own lives or experiences. That would eliminate too many wonderful poems. It does mean, however, that there must be some point of contact in the poem for the student. A student may not have experienced the death of a sibling, for example, but he or she, more than likely, has had to deal with the loss of someone close. A dear friend moves away. A beloved pet gets hit by a car. A favorite neighbor dies unexpectedly. That sense of loss could be a point of contact.

Over the years, as I've taught high school English and worked as a visiting poet in elementary and middle schools, I've developed and refined my approach to poetry. I'm still at it, but my first order of business has been, and remains, to get lots of poetry into the hands of my students. I begin that quest by finding fresh poems to share. I read new books of poetry. I reread some old ones, always on the lookout for poems that will touch my students. (As a historical aside, when I started doing this, it was well before the days when every school had at least one photocopier. It was during the golden age of the mimeograph machine, which meant that every poem I wanted to share had to be typed on a stencil then run off on a machine that, amidst whirring and thumping, shot out sheets of paper with the poems printed in purple. Those who were there know of what I speak.)

In addition to giving the students individual poems to read, I bring stacks of poetry books into the classroom. Most are mine. Some are from the public library. I escort students to the school library where they can do their own browsing and discovering.

Realizing how important it is for the students to read their poetic finds aloud and to hear them read aloud, I set class time aside for just that. Some kids say a few words about the poem, perhaps about how it spoke to them. Others read their poems and sit down. I am gratified to notice that, more and more, students ask to see one another's poems. I am happy to take part in these readings, and am always ready to read one of my own favorites.

I want my students to hear the poets themselves read their poems, so, in the past, I combed the libraries for vinyl records of poets reading their work. Despite the scratches, the records gave my students a sense of how the poet sounded reading particular poems. The tremendous advances in audio technology offer you and your students many opportunities to listen to the words of the poets. The range of authors represented on cassette and CD is staggering. (At the end of this book, I have included an annotated list of some outstanding audio programs.)

We even fool around with choral reading of one sort or another. If a poem seems to work best with groups of students reading parts in unison, we do that. Other poems sound better as two-part readings. I remember when a couple of boys read "The Raven." One of them sat at a desk, while the other, dressed in black for the occasion, perched on top of the heater, reciting the raven's immortal words. One of the most moving choral readings was when a group of kids read "I Hear America Singing" by Walt Whitman. One boy served as the narrator of the poem, while other students spoke the short part of one of the occupations that Whitman includes—carpenter, shoe-maker, and so forth.

As my students become more competent in discussing poems, our explorations become more literary. I start with small groups. Each group explores a poem and makes a brief oral presentation to the class. I choose my poems for these explo-rations very carefully. Although each group does not know what poems the other groups are assigned, all the poems are related to each other by theme or topic. It doesn't take some students long to realize that the poem one group is exploring is connect-ed to the other groups' poems. So, in addition to having the chance to study one poem's overall merit, the students discuss the relationships among the poems.

> "I want students to be readers of poetry. I want them to feel comfortable and confident reading poetry on their own. I want them to be able to talk about poetry…'"

What do I want my students to get from, as one girl put it, "all this poetry stuff"? It's a good question, and one that I have constantly asked myself during that first year and ever since. Did I want them to be scholars of poetry? Certainly not. The middle school class is not the place, nor am I the person, to take up that task. Put most simply, I want students to be readers of poetry. I want them to feel comfortable and confident reading poetry on their own. I want them to be able to talk about poetry using statements that go far beyond "I liked it" or "I hated it."

What You'll Find in This Book

The purpose of this book is to help you help your students have a richer experience when they read poetry. So, in addition to the personal history and philosophical rationale for my approach to teaching poetry, I offer practical suggestions that will serve you well when you decide to include more poetry in your classroom.

The "Explorations" section in Part 2 contains 17 poems carefully chosen for middle-school students. Each poem is accompanied by suggestions for reading that poem, with commentaries that focus on various aspects of the poem—its language, structure, and form, for example. In addition to my commentaries, which you may choose to incorporate into and adapt for your own lessons, I have included:

- a student response sheet for jotting down initial reactions to a poem, which includes thought-provoking questions and definitions of difficult vocabulary and poetic terms.
- a reproducible for each poem to help students examine it more carefully.
- background information about each poet.
- appropriate poetry web sites, including many with resources for teachers.
- suggestions for related poems to read.

Taken together, the material in each Exploration helps you bring your class alive with active and animated discussion of the poems.

Part 3 is filled with suggestions on how to become an active reader of poetry. I explore ways to weave poetry into your life and suggest resources—books, web sites, and audio books. I'm sure you'll find some old favorites among the poets and books I mention, but I hope that you also find some new ones to consider the next time you drop into the library.

PART 2:
Exploring the
Possibilities of Poetry

Whenever I present a poetry workshop for teachers, there is usually a participant who asks: "How can I get my students past the poems of Shel Silverstein and Jack Prelutsky?" If we want our students to expand their taste and interest in poetry, we must, first of all, accept where they are. We gain nothing good by dismissing the work of any poet that excites students. Beyond that, however, we must lead our students to different poetic voices, for most of them will not discover those voices on their own. As Robert Bly said, "There are poets in this country who are living like the new moon, hardly noticed."

If we value poetry and want to offer alternatives to Silverstein and Prelutsky, we must be readers of poetry ourselves. If we are not willing to read lots of poetry, we can't expect our kids to go very far beyond where they (and we) are right now. That doesn't mean we must sacrifice humor. We can read the work of J. Patrick Lewis, X.J. Kennedy, David McCord, Douglas Florian. All very funny poets, but all fine poets as well. Of course, presenting only humorous poets isn't the best way to teach poetry. We need to show kids the rich palette of poetry. Have your students read Alice Schertle, Ralph Fletcher, Naomi Shihab Nye, Nikki Grimes, and Joseph Bruchac. (I deal more extensively with finding the best poets in Part 3.)

The more poetry we read, the more comfortable we will be with it, and the more confident we will feel bringing in poems for students to share. Together with them we can explore the varieties of poetry, from rhyming poems to free verse, from classic to contemporary. We are not going to like all the poems we read. But, by reading many poems, we will come to see all that poetry has to offer. By reading many poems, we will develop our sense of what makes a good poem, for ourselves and for our students.

It is up to us to allow young people plenty of opportunities to experience poetry, to feel what Robert Francis meant when he said, "One word cannot strike sparks from itself; it takes at least two for that. It takes words lying side by side to breed wonders" (Francis, 1980). How lucky we are to see the wonders in "The Games of Night" by Nancy Willard:

The ghost comes. I don't see her.
I smell the licorice drops in her pocket.
I climb out of bed, I draw her bath.
She has come a long way, and I know she's tired.

By the light of the moon, the water splashes.
By the light of the stars, the soap leaps,
it dives, it pummels the air,
it scrubs off the dust of not-seeing,
                    [stanza break]

and I see her sandals, black like mine
and I see her dress, white like mine.
Little by little, she comes clear.
She rises up in a skin of water.

As long as the water shines, I can see her.
As long as I see her, we can play
by the light of the moon on my bed,
by the light of the stars on my bear
till the sun opens its eye, the sun that wakes things,
the sun that doesn't believe in ghosts.

How does Willard pack so much wonder into her poem? If we read the poem out loud, we will hear part of the answer. The poem is musical, from its word choice ("it scrubs off the dust of not-seeing") to its appeal to the reader's senses ("I smell the licorice drops in her pocket") to the repetition of cadences and phrases in the final stanza. Just read her last stanza aloud again and listen to the music. Are these things our students can notice? Of course…when we give them the gift of regularly reading and hearing many different poems.

Guiding Student Responses

Over 65 years ago, Louise Rosenblatt called for teachers to give students literature that is a "vital personal experience" (Rosenblatt, 1995). If reading a poem is a personal experience for our students, we can expect their first reactions to it to be personal. They might say, "I really liked the poem by Edgar Allan Poe," or "That Poe poem was a total waste of my time." We need to let our students express these initial and spontaneous responses to a poem. In *An Introduction to Poetry,* X.J. Kennedy and Dana Gioia write that the "work of a poem" is to "touch us, to stir us, to make us glad, and possibly even to tell us something" (Kennedy & Gioia, 1998). Each response from each student is as valid and acceptable as the next, as a personal and, usually, emotional reaction to the poem. Young people are often so preoccupied with their own emotional reaction to a poem that they overlook the poem itself and focus on how the poem touched them. So, it's important for us to give the students the tools to discuss the poem as a piece of writing and not merely as some sort of trigger for releasing their feelings. We must help our students grow beyond facile reactions.

We need to guide students to explore why they reacted in a particular way. What was in the poem (and in their experiences) that led them to feel about the poem the way they did? As students explore the poem this way, they begin to read poetry more thoughtfully as they look to the words in a poem for connections to their reaction. They go beyond merely stating their opinions of, for instance, "The Bells" by Edgar Allan Poe—"I liked the way you can almost hear the different bells"—to noticing *how* they can hear the different bells. They will begin to note the difference between the light and merry bells in part 1 and the heavy, almost dissonant sound of the bells in part 4. (An Exploration of this poem appears on page 75.)

In short, our students may initially react very personally and superficially to a poem. But, with encouragement and guidance from us, they will begin to look more carefully at the language, structure, and images in a poem to find the connection between the poem and their reaction to it. And, the more skilled they become in exploring a poem, the more connected to it they will feel.

So how can we can help our students explore a poem this way? Here are some suggestions:

Advocate Multiple Interpretations. We need to make certain that they do not detect in us a belief that there is one "right answer" or "standard interpretation" of a poem. We are likely to react differently to a poem at different times in our lives. Frost's "The Road Not Taken" may have been no more than a silly academic exercise when we were teenagers with the whole world before us. However, when we read that poem many years later, after we have made numerous decisions, large and small, we will more than likely see it in a new light. The poem hasn't changed. Our circumstances have changed the way we read it.

Focus on the Words. How do we get our students to react more thoughtfully to a poem? We can encourage them to focus on its words—not on the era in which the poet lived or a long list of literary terms. These things are helpful, perhaps, if students are competing on a quiz show or taking a standardized test, but, by themselves, they do not help a reader understand a poem. Rosenblatt says such information is "useless baggage" (Rosenblatt, 1995) if reading the poem is not a personal experience.

Establish a Common Vocabulary. As I mentioned, I don't want or expect my students to become scholarly explicators of the poems they read. But I do want all of us in the class to have a common vocabulary that makes it easier for us to understand each other when we explore a poem.

What concepts is it reasonable for middle school students to understand in a poem? The concepts that I consider in the next section of this book:

- **Image.** Students should have a sense of how details, word choice, and precise language create in the reader's mind an image that appeals to his or her senses.
- **Figurative Language.** Used skillfully, metaphors, similes, and personification can clarify a poet's image.
- **Rhyme.** I still run into young writers who think that a poem needs to rhyme. Rhyme can add to a poem, but if it's too heavy handed, it can ruin a poem. Students need to experience free verse poems as well as rhymed poems.
- **Repetition and Patterns.** Although rhyming poems rely more on repetition and patterns than free verse poems—mostly in end rhymes and refrains—students should see how these notions can play out in free verse as well.
- **Originality.** Good poetry says interesting things in novel ways. That novelty might come from a number of aspects of the poem, including word choice, images, structure, and metaphors. Without originality, poems are often no more than greeting card verse. As William Wordsworth said, poetry gives "the charm of novelty to things of every day."
- **Surprise.** When I read poetry, I want to be surprised. The surprise might come from the ending, but it might also come from a fresh point of view, outrageous word play, or startling images.
- **Line Break.** One of the reasons students enjoy reading and writing rhymed poems is because the end rhyme makes them feel comfortable. They need to feel equally comfortable with free verse, which comes from exploring the ways poets construct lines of poetry.
- **Rhythm.** I know many people who are captivated by poetry but cannot tell the difference between iambic hexameter and dactylic pentameter. Young students should fall into this category. In other words, they should feel the music of the line—which comes from hearing poetry read aloud—without being forced to scan the line and identify the predominate rhythm of the poem. Save that for college.

I don't quiz students on these terms, but look for them when students discuss and write about a poem. To me, it's more important for my students to discuss image and figurative language in a poem, for example, than to simply write out definitions of those terms.

If your students use these terms in their poetry discussions, they will have made that giant step from feeling the emotional impact of a poem to being able to explore how the poet worked his or her magic.

By reading many poems, young people will see that good poetry explodes with possibilities of form, language, images, structure, rhythm, voice, sound, feeling. The best teachers in the schools I visit do not proclaim April as "Poetry Month" and then ignore it the rest of the year. When I visit their classrooms, I know that my work with their students is one part of an ongoing love affair with

> "By reading many poems, young people will see that good poetry explodes with possibilities of form, language, images, structure, rhythm, voice, sound, feeling."

poetry. These teachers make poetry a part of the real world, finding poems that are related to something that happened at school, in the community, or in the world. If the poem hits the mark, the students see the connection between poetry and life. These teachers offer poems about apples in the fall, sports poems in the midst of an exciting season, or a poem about living any time.

What Students Find in the Best Poems

The best poems explode with possibilities, and we must share those possibilities with young people. Students need to recognize that poetry can mesmerize, mock, and mimic. It can celebrate, too, as "Seeing the World" by Steven Herrick does:

> Every month or so,
> when my brother and I
> are bored with backyard games
> and television, Dad says
> "It's time to see the world."
> So we climb the ladder to our attic,
> push the window open,
> and carefully, carefully
> scramble onto the roof.
> We hang on tight as we scale the heights

to the very top.
We sit with our backs to the chimney
and see the world.
The birds flying
        below us.
The trees swaying in the wind
            below us.
Our cubbyhouse, meters
          below us.
The distant city
       below us.
And then Dad, my brother, and I lie back
look up and watch
the clouds and sky
and dream
we're flying
we're flying.
In summer
with the sun and a gentle breeze
and not a sound anywhere
I'm sure I never want to land.

Your students may not have climbed to the roof with their fathers, but chances are many of them have enjoyed some memorable experiences with someone they love. That's what Herrick is writing about. Not a record-setting experience like ascending Mount Everest or pitching a no-hitter for the Red Sox. His memory is much less newsworthy, but no less spectacular to him. This memory is so precious to him, in fact, that he needed to save it in words, from his dad's invitation ("It's time to see the world") to the evocative, sensual ending of the final four lines.

Poetry can memorialize with dry humor, like my favorite epitaph, David McCord's "Epitaph on a Waiter":

By and by
God caught his eye.

Or, poetry can memorialize by showing us what Robert Francis meant when he wrote, "A poem is like an arrow; it's got to wound you." That's what I tried to do when I wrote a poem after my father died, and I was dealing with the wound of my grief. The poem is called "On the Day After My Father Died":

On the day after my father died   Wind
two mourning doves,   hissed through
pudgy spinsters   new leaves
in gray coats,   green and bright.
sat in the road and gossiped.

                                          Four hundred miles away
Lilacs,   my mother,
quiet all winter,   married to the man for 59 years,
began to whisper   sat by his chair
in violet and white.   bent with the weight
          [stanza break]   of her new silence.

At times I share Anatole Broyard's fear that we, as a society, do not read enough poetry. Writing in the *New York Times Book Review,* Broyard asked, "Where will our flair come from, our hyperbole, our *mots justes?* Unless we read poetry we'll never have our hearts broken by language, which is an indispensable preliminary to a civilized life" (Broyard, 1988). It seems to me that Broyard had in mind a poem like "Speech Class" by Jim Daniels:

We were outcasts—
you with your stutters,
me with my slurring—
and that was plenty for a friendship.

When we left class to go to the therapist
we hoped they wouldn't laugh—
took turns reminding the teacher:
"Me and Joe have to go to shpeech clash now,"

or "M-m-me and J-Jim ha-have to go to

    s-s-speech now."

Mrs. Clark, therapist, was also god, friend, mother.

Once she took us to the zoo on a field trip:

"Aw, you gonna go look at the monkeys?"

"Maybe they'll teach you how to talk."

We clenched teeth and went

and felt the sun and fed the animals

and were a family of broken words.

For years we both tried so hard

and I finally learned

where to put my tongue and how to make the sounds

and graduated,

but the first time you left class without me

I felt that punch in the gut—

I felt like a deserter

and wanted you

to have my voice.

But what do we say to the student who asks what the poet had in mind when he or she wrote a poem? That's a good question, and one, I suspect, that we've asked ourselves. The answer is, of course, that we simply cannot know what a poet has in mind when he or she writes. What we do have is the poem itself, though. And that is what we and our students must explore.

The best poems show how poetry can describe, confess, and lament. Young readers need poems that speak to them in a voice they cannot resist, as "Rites of Passage" by Dorianne Laux does:

When we were sixteen, summer nights in the suburbs sizzled

    like barbecue coals,

    the hiss of lawn sprinklers,

    telephone wires humming above our heads.

Sherry and me walked every block within five miles that year,

sneaking into backyards, peeking through windows,

we dared and double dared each other from behind the redwood slats.

Frog-legged, we slid down street lamps,

our laughter leaving trails of barking dogs behind us.

One night we came home the back way,

perfecting sexy walks and feeling "cool,"

and found my little sister on the side porch,

hiding behind the plastic trash bins in her nightgown,

smoking Salems,

making Monroe faces in a hand-held mirror.

Consider the image that Laux creates in this poem. With about a hundred words, she gives us an image that is built on her sense impressions. The poem opens with the sounds of summer. Then Laux serves up the visual image of action, the narrator and her friend "sneaking into back yards, peeking through windows." We can see the girls "frog-legged," sliding down street lamps. We can hear their laughter, as well as the "trail of barking dogs" they leave in their wake. These young girls are "perfecting sexy walks and feeling 'cool'" when they suddenly find the younger sister "smoking Salems" and working on her Marilyn Monroe faces in a hand mirror. We can sense the shift in mood near the end of the poem as the narrator realizes that her sister is growing up, that she is going through a rite of passage. And, yet, by realizing this, isn't the narrator going through her own rite of passage?

The best poems ask questions we all ask. They are like life itself. They celebrate the grace of little things. Billy Collins thinks there is a "very basic need" to get back to poetry, "perhaps in some kind of spiritual sense, but also just as a brief form of verbal engagement and entertainment with another consciousness, and also with your own consciousness" (Whited, 2001).

The best poems are alive with intense, inventive language. Mark Twain said that the difference between the right word and the almost right word is like the difference between *lightning* and *lightning bug*. And nowhere is that more obvious than in poetry where word choice is crucial. Poems can provoke, praise, and remember. Above all, young readers need to know that poetry sings of human experiences, very often their own experiences, as in this poem by Joanne Ryder called "Enchantment":

On warm summer nights
the porch becomes our living room
where Mama takes her reading
and Dad and I play games
in the patch of brightness
the lamp scatters on the floor.
From the darkness, others come—
small round bodies
clinging to the screens

which separate us
from the yard beyond.
Drawn to our light,
the June bugs watch our games
and listen to our talk till bedtime
when Mama darkens the porch
and breaks the spell
that holds them close to us.

Like Laux, Joanne Ryder has chosen the perfect title for her poem because she does a masterful job of selected details that set a relaxed and comfortable mood in this poem. We can imagine this family, safe in the "patch of brightness/the lamp scatters on the floor": the narrator and her dad playing a game, the mom reading. To complete the picture, "the June bugs watch our games/and listen to our talk till bedtime." Then, true to the title of the poem, Mama "breaks the spell" when she "darkens the porch."

Ryder's word choice carries the poem. Instead of writing about a *patch of light,* she writes "a patch of brightness." The light from the lamp "scatters on the floor." The "round bodies" of the evening bugs are "clinging to the screens." And it is her word choice that creates the feeling of contentment that the poet recalls.

I want young readers to see that poetry is accessible, that it's something that captures experiences, holds the meanings in life, and communicates with language wild and marvelous. I want students to know that poems can narrate, provoke, console, and even commemorate, like Paul Zimmer's poem, "Zimmer's Head Thudding Against the Blackboard":

> At the blackboard I had missed
> Five number problems in a row,
> And was about to foul a sixth,
> When the old, exasperated nun
> Began to pound my head against

> "I want young readers to see that poetry is accessible, that it's something that captures experiences, holds the meanings in life, and communicates with language wild and marvelous."

My six mistakes. When I cried,
She threw me back into my seat,
Where I hid my head and swore
That very day I'd be a poet,
And curse her yellow teeth with this.

Readers who lose themselves in good poetry will quickly feel that the best poems are rich with the textures of life. By reading poetry, we come to see that each poem has a purpose, as Jonathan Holden describes well, "to give shape, in a concise and memorable way, to what our lives feel like… Poems help us to notice the world more and better, and they enable us to share with others" (Janeczko, 1983). And that's exactly what Cathy Young Czapla does in "Carpenter's Daughter":

I always woke to
bedrooms marked off with masking tape and
the smell of joint compound mixed with mountain
air. The tools all knew their proper names—
blue chalk-line, straight-claw hammer, level,
steel tape, combination square and bench vise.
I learned to respect the circular saw and
the man—the power behind it. I learned
all the textures of sawdust.
I learned my mother's fears—
falling ladders,
slippery roofs,
the momentary lapse in attention that
took off the tip of one finger,

the storm
when lightning scratched blue lines
through falling snow, and the wind
picked up the sheetmetal roofing
and carried it over my father's head.

Czapla notices the world "more and better" through her senses. We can see the masking tape on the bedroom floor. We can smell the joint compound. We can feel "all the textures of sawdust." But we can also feel what she feels in her gut—"I learned my mother's fears—" the dangers of "falling ladders,/slippery roofs" and the sheetmetal roofing sailing over her father's head in the wind. If we can feel this poem, we sense that Molly Peacock was right when she said that we become attracted to a poem because "it makes us feel as if someone is listening to us…the voice of the poem allows us to hear ourselves" (Peacock, 1999).

Philip Booth said that a good poem "makes the world more habitable." Any good poem, he went on to say, "changes the world. It changes the world slightly in favor of being alive and being human" (Dunn, 1986). That, in itself, may be the most important reason to share poetry with students. Poetry can give all of us a chance to be human. A chance to see all we have in common as residents of this planet. Lucille Clifton gives readers a chance to consider the importance of belonging in her poem "in the inner city":

in the inner city

or

like we call it

home

we think a lot about uptown

and the silent nights

and the houses straight as

dead men

and the pastel lights

and we hang on to our place

happy to be alive

and in the inner city

or

like we call it

home

All young readers deserve a chance to be touched by a poem. As award-winning poet Stanley Kunitz said, if we listen hard enough to poets, "who knows—we too may break into dance, perhaps for grief, perhaps for joy" (Heard, 1989).

Introduction to Explorations

The Explorations that follow are designed to make poetry reading an interactive experience between each student and poem and among the members of your class. They contain response sheets and reproducibles, which students will most likely do on their own, as well as commentaries that encourage audience participation. And, as you know, once students start sharing their opinions and insights, the discussions can become intense. Just what you want!

The poems are not in any sort of sequential order, because what might be an accessible poem for one class can be troublesome for another. Use the Concept Chart on pages 30–31, which categorizes each poem by term and concept, to help you decide on a suitable order.

Preparation

I created the Explorations for teachers who want to do extraordinary work in an ordinary classroom with ordinary supplies (or lack thereof). They're pretty low tech. No *PowerPoint* required, though an overhead projector and audiocassette player might help. Since students are apt to encounter words they may not understand, you might want to have some dictionaries on hand, too.

Before you present one of the poems to your class, read it once. Read it twice. And even a third time. The commentaries and activities that follow it will make more sense if you are familiar with the poem. Come to the poem with a beginner's mind. Even if you've read the poem before, be open to it. Let yourself be surprised by it. Make observations in a poetry journal. Take notes. Underline. Draw boxes, arrows, and circles to show connections, contradictions, and colossal moments.

Try to imagine how your students might feel when they read the poem for the first time. Can you anticipate their reactions to the poem? Any reservations they might have? Is there a way you can deal with those reactions ahead of time? Perhaps, for example, some vocabulary might present a problem. Although I've included definitions of some potentially troublesome words in the student response sheets, you may notice others. You might write them on the board and discuss them before you hand out the poem.

Presentation

Each Exploration begins with "openers," questions to pose to the class before your students look at the poem, to get them thinking about some of its issues or themes. From there, with a few exceptions, the Explorations follow a consistent sequence that I encourage you to modify as you see fit.

Once you've discussed the openers as a class, distribute the student response sheet and review the "As You Read" section, which contains definitions of challenging vocabulary words and other things to think about to help students get the most out of the poem.

From there, hand out the poem and have at least two student volunteers read it aloud so that the class hears different interpretations. You might even allow the volunteers time and space in the room to practice reading the poem to a few friends before reading it to the entire class. Be sure to give students a few reminders about how to read a poem, such as not stopping at the end of each line unless punctuation dictates.

When students have had a chance to hear the poem read at least a couple of times, refer them to the "After You Read" section, which contains two questions, among others:

1. What did you notice about the poem? Mark up your poem with underlines, circles, and arrows to show what you noticed.

This question gives students the freedom to encounter the poem at their own level. Some students will notice rhyme schemes or alliteration. Others will notice how all of the lines begin with a capital letter. Anything goes. Regardless of the sophistication of the observations, allow students the luxury of entering the poem in a way that feels comfortable to them. You'll get a variety of responses. Be open to them as observations about the poem, but not gospel.

2. Do you have any questions about this poem? Jot them down.

This questions gives students a chance to think out loud on paper. Let students know that it's okay to ask any questions. Will you have all the answers? Certainly not. But, as we know, sometimes the questions can be more important than the answers. Not all their questions will have answers, for example, "Why did the poet do that?" We can make educated guesses, but we need to accept the uncertainty that comes with a less-than-definitive answer. And, bear in mind, a question asked in October might find its answer in a poem read in May. Encourage your students to be open to some of the ambiguities in poetry (and in life).

Each Exploration also includes a reproducible that gives students another opportunity to interact with the poem either on their own before or as they are discussing it as a class.

Once students have read the poem and investigated it on their own terms, discuss it as a class. The bulk of each Exploration is made up of commentaries that focus on various aspects of the

Concept Chart

	Figurative Language	Originality	Image	Word Choice	The Ending	Details	Sound	Repetition
1. "Ode to Pablo's Tennis Shoes"	•	•						
2. "Cottontail"			•	•	•			
3. "Old Florist"						•	•	•
4. "A Little Girl's Poem"						•	•	•
5. "The Red Gloves"	•		•				•	
6. "The Telling Tree"			•	•				
7. "A Room in the Past"	•					•	•	
8. "The Bells"							•	
9. "Famous"				•		•	•	
10. "Wintered Sunflowers"	•			•			•	
11. "Lullaby"						•		
12. "Miracles"				•			•	•
13. Three Short Poems			•			•		
14. "Remember"								•
15. "Noise"				•			•	

Rhythm	Character	Subject	Mood	Implications	Poems as a Group	Structure	Form	Persona Poem	Narrative Poem	Sonnet	Ode	List Poem	Free Verse
			•	•			•				•		
•							•		•				
		•											
						•							
						•	•	•					
						•							
	•												
						•							•
			•			•						•	
						•	•					•	•
					•		•						
						•	•			•			
						•							

poem—its language, structure, and form, for example. Use these commentaries as I present them here or adapt them. Remember, the Explorations are meant as a topographical map to help you guide your students through the terrain of individual poems. But, as any true explorer will tell you, you need to be ready to step off the beaten path when an interesting possibility presents itself. Be ready to seize the opportunity when it beckons. Take the risk. Have faith in your students. You never know what will happen. It could be magical, more magical than following a lesson plan. Don't use my suggestions and activities verbatim. You know your students. I don't. You know what will work with them and what won't. Trust your instincts.

You might want to consider having your students work in pairs for some of the Explorations, especially if they seem timid about reading poetry and sharing their reactions.

I conclude each Exploration with a section called "Related Poems," which contains a few poems that connect somehow to the main poem. Sometimes that connection is thematic. Other times it has more to do with language and form. These poems enable you to extend the lesson or give students more experience exploring the ideas you've discussed.

Explorations are not meant to cover everything about these poems. You and your students will surely find more to say, which is as it should be. Just as my commentaries are not meant to be exhaustive, neither is my method for approaching a poem. Again, I trust you will find your own way to read poems as you work your way through the Explorations. I hope you make many marvelous discoveries along the way.

"Ode to Pablo's Tennis Shoes"

Gary Soto

They wait under Pablo's bed,
Rain-beaten, sun-beaten,
A scuff of green
At their tips
From when he fell
In the school yard.
He fell leaping for a football
That sailed his way.
But Pablo fell and got up,
Green on his shoes,
With the football
Out of reach.

Now it's night.
Pablo is in bed listening
To his mother laughing
to the Mexican *novelas* on TV.
His shoes, twin pets
That snuggle his toes,
Are under the bed.
He should have bathed,
But he didn't.
(Dirt rolls from his palm,
Blades of grass
Tumble from his hair.)

He wants to be
Like his shoes,
A little dirty
From the road,
A little worn
From racing to the drinking fountain
A hundred times in one day.
It takes water
To make him go,
And his shoes to get him
There. He loves his shoes,
Cloth like a sail,
Rubber like
A lifeboat on rough sea.
Pablo is tired,
Sinking into the mattress.
His eyes sting from
Grass and long words in books.
He needs eight hours
Of sleep
To cool his shoes,
The tongues hanging
Out, exhausted.

"Ode to Pablo's Tennis Shoes"
Gary Soto

Some of your students might be surprised that a poet could write a poem about a pair of dirty tennis shoes. They might ask, "What's so important about a pair of tennis shoes?" In "Ode to Pablo's Tennis Shoes," Gary Soto shows us that these shoes are, indeed, quite important to Pablo. And, by focusing on details and making some telling comparisons, Soto elevates these tennis shoes in a way that will have many readers understanding that they are not just another pair of sneakers.

OPENERS Before reading the poem, have students:

1. List a few everyday, common things for which they are grateful.
2. Pick one of their "common things" and explain why it's important to them.

- Distribute the poem and have students read it silently and then in pairs or small groups. Pick at least two volunteers to read the poem to the entire class.
- Distribute the Response Sheet 1 on page 37. Ask students to answer the questions and review the poetic terms.
- Explore the poem with your class by focusing on:

FORM

The ode is a poem that celebrates a subject. It has a venerable history, going back to Pindar and Horace in ancient Greece. Pindar's odes were meant to be sung and danced in a theater. Horace's, on the other hand, were more meditative and contemplative. Odes were quite popular with the English Romantic poets. Among the more famous odes from the period are: "Ode to a Nightingale" and "Ode to a Grecian Urn" by John Keats, "Dejection: An Ode" by Samuel Taylor Coleridge, and "Ode to the West Wind" and "To a Skylark" by Percy Bysshe Shelley.

Originally, the ode was dignified and written in exalted language. Over time, however, poets have relinquished such formality. One of the more prolific writers of odes is Chilean poet Pablo Neruda, who wrote three books of odes, the best of which are collected in the bilingual edition of *Selected Odes of Pablo Neruda* (University of California Press, 1990). With its informality and exuberance, Gary Soto's "Ode to Pablo's Tennis Shoes" is a good example of a contemporary ode.

MOOD

One of the things that any good writer does is establish a mood in a piece of writing. How does the piece make you feel? Scared or sad or angry, perhaps? After your students have read the poem to themselves or have heard a classmate or two read it aloud, you might ask them: How did you feel when you read "Ode to Pablo's Tennis Shoes"? How do you think Pablo feels?

Soto creates a feeling of relaxation after an active day of "leaping for a football." Pablo is resting, while his tennis shoes "wait under Pablo's bed." The boy is "listening/To his mother laughing" as she watches the Mexican soap operas on television. His tennis shoes, "that snuggle his toes,/Are under his bed." He's not bathed, which suggests he has just tumbled into bed. He wants to be "A little worn," like the shoes that "He loves." Pablo "is tired/Sinking into the mattress." The boy is ready for the eight hours of sleep that he needs.

IMPLICATIONS

HAND OUT REPRODUCIBLE **1** According to the title, this poem is about Pablo's tennis shoes. And it delivers. We get to see these tennis shoes quite well. However, the poem does not give us much direct information about Pablo. But, like so many good poems, it implies a number of things about him. Give your students Reproducible 1 and ask them to read the poem to themselves and jot down things that they learn about Pablo and give the evidence that led them to their conclusions. For example, even though the poet doesn't tell us that Pablo is active, the first stanza does show us an active kid.

FIGURATIVE LANGUAGE

If your students are unfamiliar with some of the basic forms of figurative language—non-literal expressions to get across certain images or ideas more vividly—this ode gives them a chance to explore them. Ask students to circle any places in the poem where Soto compares one thing to another. See if they can notice a difference in the way he compares things. Your students may notice, for example, that the poet refers to Pablo's shoes as his "twin pets" in line 17. They are likely to notice how Soto uses a different kind of comparison in lines 36 to 38 to describe the shoes: "Cloth like a sail,/Rubber like/A lifeboat on rough sea."

When your students can see these two comparisons, you can explain how the first comparison, in which the poet makes a direct comparison, is a metaphor. The second example is a simile because the poet uses *like* (or *as*) in his comparison. Metaphors and similes are the backbone of poetry because they help the reader see more clearly similarities between the ideas and images being compared.

ORIGINALITY

Originality helps a good poem stand apart from greeting card verse. A good poem says what it needs to say in a fresh way. The language is original. The images are original. In the case of "Ode to Pablo's Tennis Shoes," Soto skillfully shows that a couple of the qualities that Pablo admires in the tennis shoes are the same qualities that he possesses.

To help students see the comparison between the boy and his tennis shoes, have them read the poem carefully for connections. In lines 25 and 26, for example, Soto says that Pablo:

> ...wants to be
> Like his shoes,
> A little dirty
> From the road,
> A little worn
> From racing to the drinking fountain

But Soto also points out, "Pablo is tired" and so are his shoes, as they rest under his bed, "The tongues hanging/Out, exhausted." The boy "needs eight hours/Of sleep/To cool his shoes," but he also needs that time to cool himself for a new day of running around with his fabulous tennis shoes.

RELATED POEMS

"Ode to a Stamp Album," Pablo Neruda
"Ode to My Socks," Pablo Neruda
"String," Valerie Worth

Focus on the Poet

This ode is part of Gary Soto's *Neighborhood Odes* (Harcourt, 1992). Two other Soto collections for young readers are *Canto Familiar* (Harcourt, 1995) and *A Fire in My Hands* (Scholastic, 1990), which include Soto's comments on the poems. If you are interested in reading Soto's poems for adults, look for his *New and Selected Poems* (Chronicle Books, 1995).

You and your students can visit <www.garysoto.com> to find out more about him. You can also find an autobiographical sketch of Soto, as well as other information about him, by clicking on "Online Activities Center" at <http://teacher.scholastic.com/>, then click on "Authors & Books."

Name: _____ Date: _____

"Ode To Pablo's Tennis Shoes"
Gary Soto

1. What did you notice about "Ode to Pablo's Tennis Shoes"? Mark up the poem with underlines, circles, and arrows to show what you noticed.

2. Do you have any questions about this poem? Jot them down.

_____

_____

_____

_____

3. **Helpful Vocabulary**: Based on the way the Spanish word *novelas* is used in the poem, can you make an educated guess about what it means?

Poetic Terms

Here are some terms that will help you talk about the poem:

ode: a poem that celebrates a subject

mood: the atmosphere in a piece of writing

figurative language: non-literal expressions to get across certain ideas or things more vividly

metaphor: a comparison of dissimilar things that implies some sort of equality between the things

simile: a comparison that uses "like" or "as"

Name: _____   Date: _____

"Ode to Pablo's Tennis Shoes"
Gary Soto

If you read Soto's poem carefully, you can learn a lot about Pablo. In some cases, the poet may give us information directly. At other times, he may imply information about a subject. In the left column, write what you learn about Pablo from reading the poem. In the right column, write down evidence from the poem that supports your statements.

What You Learned About Pablo	Evidence

Opening a Door • Scholastic Professional Books

"Cottontail"
George Bogin

A couple of kids,
we went hunting for woodchucks
fifty years ago
in a farmer's field.
No woodchucks
but we cornered
a terrified
little cottontail rabbit
in the angle
of two stone fences.
He was sitting up,
front paws together,
supplicating,
trembling,
while we were deciding
whether to shoot him
or spare him.
I shot first
but missed,
thank God.

Then my friend fired
and killed him
and burst into tears.
I did too.
A little cottontail.
A haunter.

"Cottontail"
George Bogin

Many young writers have the mistaken notion that to write a good poem they need to have a dramatic and impressive story to tell. They feel that their lives are too dull to be of interest to readers. While their lives may not have the excitement of a comic book hero's, they are filled with events that touch their hearts. And young poets should write about those moments. They will find that, if they do a good job of writing about a personally significant event, they will touch the reader.

OPENERS Before reading the poem, have students:

1. Name a couple of things they didn't really want to do, but did anyway, maybe because of peer pressure.
2. Think of two things they've done in life that they regret.

HAND OUT REPRODUCIBLE 2 Distribute Reproducible 2 on page 44 and ask students to briefly describe two events in their lives that affected them deeply, even if only for a short time. These events need not be spectacular enough to make the front page of the newspaper.

- Distribute Response Sheet 2 on page 43 and ask students to review the "words to know" in the "As You Read" section.
- Distribute the poem and have students read it silently and then in pairs or small groups. Pick at least two volunteers to read the poem to the entire class.
- Have students complete the "After You Read" section of Response Sheet 2.
- Explore the poem with your class by focusing on:

FORM

George Bogin's poem is a narrative, a poem that tells a story. And his story is quite short: 26 lines, about 90 words. With those 90 words he tells a story about an event that, if we are to take him at his word, happened 50 years before he wrote the poem. Ask a student to tell you what happens in the poem. What is the main event? Your student will probably tell you that the poem is a story of two boys who corner and shoot a rabbit. And that retelling will probably not be much shorter than the event was itself. Yet the event had such an impact on Bogin that he felt compelled to write about it so many years later. This zeroing in on one small but heart-touching event is the essence of writing a good narrative poem. Ask your students if one of the events they wrote about on Reproducible 2 might make a good poem.

IMAGE

Poets create images with words. Clear, precise words that put the reader in their shoes. How does Bogin create his image? For one thing, he starts the poem off in something of a breezy fashion, telling how he and a friend were "hunting for woodchucks...in a farmer's field." See if your class notices how the scene and mood change in line 6 as the image sharpens: "we cornered/a terrified/little cottontail rabbit." The rabbit is helpless before these two young hunters. In line 10 Bogin shows us more about the rabbit: "He was sitting up,/front paws together,/ supplicating,/ trembling." What picture does he paint for us? Do your students notice how Bogin describes the rabbit? The helpless creature is almost begging for mercy, begging to be spared. Nine words in four lines give a very clear picture of that frightened rabbit.

After Bogin shows us the boys' intended victim, he switches to show us the feelings of the boys, after they decide to shoot the rabbit. Ask your students how the narrator feels when he misses. They should notice his relief after he misses his shot: "thank God." His friend is not as lucky. He kills the rabbit and "burst into tears." The callous act affects the narrator, who also bursts into tears.

WORD CHOICE: TITLE

Some poem titles simply describe what the poem is about. But other titles, like "Cottontail," go beyond that without giving away the poem. Like a good poem, a good title suggests. Ask your students why they think Bogin named his poem "Cottontail." Most of them will consider the answer a no-brainer. "He named it 'Cottontail,'" they'll probably tell you, "because that's what the poem's about." Then why didn't he simply call it "Rabbit"? After saying the title aloud a few times, many of them will come to recognize that "Cottontail" is a softer word than "rabbit," thus connoting a image of softness and cuteness and helplessness, which makes the boys' action in the poem that much more deplorable.

RHYTHM

As your students read "Cottontail" aloud, they may notice that most of its lines are very short, which makes it a good poem to compare to Walt Whitman's "Miracles," with its long sprawling lines, which appears on page 101. In addition, about half the lines end with punctuation that tells us to pause at the end. Can your students hear the halting quality of those lines, almost as if the poet is having a hard time telling his story? This feeling seems strongest in the last six lines, especially in the final three, where each line only contains two or three words and is stopped by a period.

THE ENDING

Maxine Kumin said that the end of a poem should be like the sound of a door clicking shut. And that is exactly what the last line of this poem is: a fitting ending to a story about a horrible childhood indiscretion. But, although this ending closes the telling of the story, it doesn't really close the poem because the poet is haunted by his action 50 years later.

Although there is a lot about this poem that I like, the final two lines, a mere five words, are the perfect ending for the poem. Bogin mentions fragility of the victim—"A little cotton-tail"—and then the clincher: "A haunter." To me that final line echoes in my heart long after I finish reading the poem.

RELATED POEMS

"Jump," Jo Carson
"Swinging the River," Charles Harper Webb
"Nightmares," Angela Johnson

Focus on the Poet

Unfortunately, when George Bogin died in 1988, he had published but one book of his poems, *In a Surf of Strangers*. I've been lucky enough to have included his work in a few of my anthologies, so you can look to them for more poems by this wonderful poet:

Wherever Home Begins (Orchard Books, 1995): "Home" and "Troopship for France, War II"

The Music of What Happens (Orchard Books, 1988): "The Kiss," "Cottontail," and "Martha Nelson Speaks"

Going Over to Your Place (Simon & Schuster, 1987): "Abraham"

I Feel a Little Jumpy Around You (Simon & Schuster, 1996): "Nineteen"

Name: _____ Date: _____

"Cottontail"
George Bogin

AS YOU READ

Words to Know: Here are two words that are important in the poem.

> *supplicating:* begging

> *spare:* to refrain from harming

AFTER YOU READ

Answer these questions:

1. What did you notice about "Cottontail"? Mark up the poem with underlines, circles, and arrows to show what you noticed.

2. Do you have any questions about the poem? Jot them down.

_____

_____

_____

_____

Poetic Terms

Here are some terms that will help you talk about the poem:

narrative poem: a poem that tells a story

image: the picture that a poem creates with vivid words that appeal to the reader's senses

rhythm: the basic beat in a line of poetry

Name: _____   Date: _____

"Cottontail"
George Bogin

In the boxes below, briefly describe two events in your life that affected you deeply, even if only for a short time.

<table>
<tr><td></td><td></td></tr>
</table>

"Old Florist"
Theodore Roethke

That hump of a man bunching chrysanthemums

Or pinching-back asters, or planting azaleas,

Tamping and stamping dirt into pots,—

How he could flick and pick

Rotten leaves or yellow petals,

Or scoop out a weed close to flourishing roots,

Or make the dust buzz with a light spray,

Or drown a bug in one spit of tobacco juice,

Or fan life into wilted sweet-peas with his hat,

Or stand all night watering roses, his feet blue in rubber boots.

"Old Florist"
Theodore Roethke

This is another poem that celebrates the ordinary in our lives. But, whereas "Cottontail" examines a single event, "Old Florist" examines a single person as he goes about the business of being a florist. It sings with the words that Roethke carefully chose to include. Roethke shows how a poet may choose a word because of the action it shows. Or maybe because of the sound it makes. Or maybe because of a detail it conveys that enriches the poem.

OPENERS Before reading the poem, have students:

1. Name an interesting relative, neighbor, or someone they know who works in a store.
2. List two or three things about that person that makes him or her interesting.

- Distribute Response Sheet 3 on page 49 and ask students to review the "As You Read" section.
- Distribute the poem and have students read it silently and then in pairs or small groups. Pick at least two volunteers to read the poem to the entire class.
- Have students complete the "After You Read" section of Response Sheet 3.
- Explore the poem with your class by focusing on:

DETAILS

In the very first line of the poem, Roethke provides details that create an image of the old florist, that "hump of a man bunching chrysanthemums." Roethke ends the poem with the vivid detail of the man's feet "blue in rubber boots." But between those opening and closing lines, the poem is alive with details. Specific flowers are mentioned: roses, chrysanthemums, asters, azaleas, sweet-peas. Ask your students if they are familiar with these flowers. Can they give you any details of color, size, shape?

HAND OUT REPRODUCIBLE **3** This florist is a man of action. Roethke was not content to have him simply "picking flowers." Give your students Reproducible 3 on page 50 and ask them to write some of the expressive words that show what the florist does. Hopefully, they will notice action details such as bunching, pinching-back, planting, tamping, stamping. Line four begins a litany of actions that the old florist has been known to do, captured by the poet in precise words. The florist flicks, picks, scoops out a weed, makes the dust buzz, drowns a bug, fans life, and stands all night watering roses. Roethke's specific details not only create the man, but they put him into action before the reader's eyes.

SOUND

If your students have read the poem aloud a few times, they will undoubtedly notice how Roethke chose words for their sounds. Ask students if they can find pairs of words that have similar sounds. They may notice some of these:

- the *uh* sound in *hump* and *bunching* in line 1
- the rhyme of *Tamping* and *stamping* in line 3
- the rhyme of *flick* and *pick* in line 4
- the *oo* sound in *scoop* and *roots* in line 6, as well as in *boots* in the last line
- the *uh* sound in *dust* and *buzz* in line 7
- the *b* in *blue* and *rubber boots* in line 10

After your students have noticed some of these sounds, explain that the repetition of vowel sounds in words is called assonance. Repetition of an initial consonant sound is called alliteration. Onomatopoeia refers to words that sound like their meaning, for example, *hiss, splat, bang,* and *boing.* In this poem, *buzz* is an example of onomatopoeia. I would include *flick* in that category as well.

REPETITION

Roethke also uses the repetition of the word *or* to serve as a refrain of sorts that stitches the poem together. The small word appears eight times in the poem. It appears in every line beginning with line 5 and, in fact, is the first word of lines 6 to 10, where it's always followed by a verb. The repetition of *or* and a verb helps create a rhythmic flow. Have your students read the poem aloud a few times and see if they can hear the rhythm.

THE SUBJECT OF THE POEM

As I mentioned at the start of this Exploration, this poem celebrates the ordinary in our lives. Your students need to be reminded that a good poem need not be written about "the spectacular." Rather, the best poems are often about the things we see and feel every day. A good poet can take an ordinary person, as Roethke did with his old florist, and make that person come alive for his readers. A good poet can bring a person or a scene to life, then preserve it so we can return to it every time we read the poem. That's what George Bogin did with "Cottontail." Remind your students that a poem does not have to have some hidden meaning that only a few "really smart" kids can figure out. A good poem gives us the chance to see what the poet saw and to feel what he felt.

RELATED POEMS

"Grandmother's Spit," Andrew Hudgins
"White on White," Christine Hemp
"Field Trip," Nikki Grimes

Focus on the Poet

"Big Wind," "Elegy for Jane," and "My Papa's Waltz" are some other poems by Theodore Roethke that you and your students might enjoy. All of them can be found in *The Collected Poems of Theodore Roethke* (Doubleday, 1983). Roethke is one of the poets included in *Eight American Poets: An Anthology*, edited by Joel Conarroe (Vintage, 1997).

Name: _____   Date: _____

"Old Florist"
Theodore Roethke

AS YOU READ

1. Be on the lookout for action words that show what the florist can do.

2. **Words to Know:** You probably know all the words in this poem, except perhaps some of the flower names. Here are three that you should know because they add color to the poem:

   • chrysanthemum

   • aster

   • azalea

AFTER YOU READ

Answer these questions:

1. What did you notice about "Old Florist"? Mark up the poem with underlines, circles, and arrows to show what you noticed.

2. Do you have any questions about the poem? Jot them down.

_____

_____

_____

_____

Poetic Terms

Here are some terms that will help you talk about the poem:

onomatopoeia: a word that makes the sound of the action it describes

alliteration: repetition of an initial consonant sound

assonance: repetition of vowel sounds in words

Name: _____ Date: _____

"Old Florist"
Theodore Roethke

In each of the six boxes below, write in a word or phrase from the poem that the poet uses to show what the "Old Florist" does.

"A Little Girl's Poem"

Gwendolyn Brooks

Life is for me and is shining!
Inside me I
feel stars and sun and bells singing.

There are children in the world
all around me and beyond me—
here, and beyond the big waters;
here, and in countries peculiar to me
but not peculiar to themselves.

I want the children to live and to laugh.
I want them to sit with their mothers and fathers
and have happy cocoa together.

I do not want
fire screaming up to the sky.
I do not want
families killed in their doorways.

Life is for us, for the children.
Life is for mothers and fathers,
life is for the tall girls and boys
in the high school on Henderson Street,
is for the people in Afrikan tents,
the people in English cathedrals,
the people in Indian courtyards;
the people in cottages all over the world.

Life is for us, and is shining.
We have a right to sing.

"A Little Girl's Poem"
Gwendolyn Brooks

Gwendolyn Brooks is such a skillful poet of sound. Many of her poems, like "We Real Cool," carry with them a jazz-like bebop quality when read aloud. "A Little Girl's Poem" is a good example of how a poet uses words to create sounds in a poem. In fact, she nearly creates a prayer-like tone with its sounds and rhythms.

OPENERS Before reading the poem, ask students:

1. If you could change anything about the world, what would it be?
2. What would your "ideal" life be like?

- Distribute Response Sheet 4 on page 55 and ask students to review the "As You Read" section.
- Distribute the poem and have students read it silently and then in pairs or small groups. Pick at least two volunteers to read the poem to the entire class.
- Have students complete the "After You Read" section of Response Sheet 4.
- Explore the poem with your class by focusing on:

SOUND

After the first two stanzas of this poem, Brooks uses repetition to join one part of the poem to the next, which carries us along. For example, in the third stanza, she repeats the phrase "I want," then quickly builds on it in the next stanza by repeating the phrase "I do not want." Both phrases are clear and forceful. In the fifth stanza, the longest in the poem, she includes the phrase "Life is for" three times for emphasis. In the second half of that stanza she uses the phrase "the people" four times. Through this repetition, we sense the little girl is standing tall and speaking firmly about what she wants for the world, not just for herself.

Although it's always good to read poems aloud, certain poems cry out for us to do a little more than that. "A Little Girl's Poem" strikes me as that sort of poem. It's a good poem to perform as a choral reading. You might want to have one student play the part of the primary narrator of the poem, reading the first two stanzas. From that point, have that student read only the repeated phrases and have other students read the rest of the lines, individually or in small groups.

Here's what stanzas three and four might sound like:

- Student 1: I want
- Student 2 (or small group): the children to live and to laugh.
- Student 1: I want
- Student 2 (or group): to sit with their mothers and fathers/and have happy cocoa together.

- Student 1: I do not want
- Student 2 (or group): fire screaming up to the sky.
- Student 1: I do not want
- Student 2 (or group): families killed in their doorways.

    Stanza five could work in a similar way. Don't be afraid to try different configurations. Maybe have small groups read different sections, with no individual readers. If you try different readings, record them on a cassette and play them back to the class. Spend some time talking with your students about how different readings affect the way they hear the poem.

DETAILS

If this poem merely repeated some catchy phrases, it would not be the poem that it is. Brooks uses details to complete the phrases that she repeats. Ask your students to look at stanza three to see that she wants "the children to live and to laugh." There are other, more specific details in that stanza. The narrator wants them "to sit with their mothers and fathers/and have happy cocoa together." Ask your students how the next stanza—which repeats the phrase "I do not want"—contrasts with the peaceful and happy details in stanza three. The narrator of the poem does not want "fire screaming up to the sky" or "families killed in their doorways."

STRUCTURE

HAND OUT REPRODUCIBLE **4**   Although the poet begins the poem by saying "Life is for me," she broadens her view in the fifth stanza, where she includes other people that deserve a good life. Give your students a few minutes to fill in Reproducible 4 on page 56 with details that show what the narrator would include in this peaceful life. Not only does she include people close to her own life—children, mothers, fathers, and "tall girls and boys/in the high school on Henderson Street," but she also includes people from around the world. Life is for "the people in Afrikan tents… in English cathedrals… in Indian courtyards… in cottages all over the world."

THE ENDING

Students need to remember that the end of a poem is very important. Ask them what they notice about the ending of "A Little Girl's Poem." Chances are they'll notice how the final two lines echo the first three lines of the poem, but with an important difference. The little girl begins by focusing on herself. She says "Life is for me…" and "Inside me I/feel stars and sun and bells singing." But by the end of the poem, her emphasis has changed to include others. The pronouns are now plural: "Life is for us…" and "We have a right to sing." Her journey through the poem has allowed her to see beyond what she wants for herself. The final two lines of the poem emphasize that.

RELATED POEMS

"Life Doesn't Frighten Me," Maya Angelou
"The Nub of the Nation," Eve Merriam
"Diner," Janet S. Wong

Focus on the Poet

Gwendolyn Brooks (1917–2000) was a prolific author, writing poems, essays, reviews, and fiction. Nonetheless, she is best known for her poetry. With subject matter drawn from her experiences in the black neighborhoods of Chicago, Brooks' second collection, *Annie Allen*, won the Pulitzer Prize for poetry in 1950. Her other books of poetry include *A Street in Bronzeville* (Harper & Row, 1945), *Maude Martha* (1953), *Bronzeville Boys and Girls* (1956), and *In the Mecca* (1968). With the death of Carl Sandburg in 1967, Brooks was selected as Poet Laureate of Illinois, a position she held until her death.

You can find substantial online information about her at <www.english.uiuc.edu/maps/index.htm> under "Poets."

Name: _____   Date: _____

"A Little Girl's Poem"
Gwendolyn Brooks

AS YOU READ

1. Think about what the poet is asking from life.

2. **Words to Know:** Here are two important words in the poem:

   peculiar: unusual or odd; eccentric

   cathedral: the principal church in a diocese

AFTER YOU READ

Answer these questions:

1. What did you notice about "A Little Girl's Poem"? Mark up the poem with underlines, circles, and arrows to show what you noticed.

2. Do you have any questions about the poem? Jot them down.

_____

_____

_____

_____

Poetic Term

Here is a term that will help you talk about the poem:

refrain: a word or phrase in a poem or song that is repeated throughout, frequently at regular intervals

---

Name: _____   Date: _____

"A Little Girl's Poem"
Gwendolyn Brooks

After carefully reading "A Little Girl's Poem," use the diagram below to record:

- what the narrator wants in her life
- what she doesn't want
- who she would include in this life

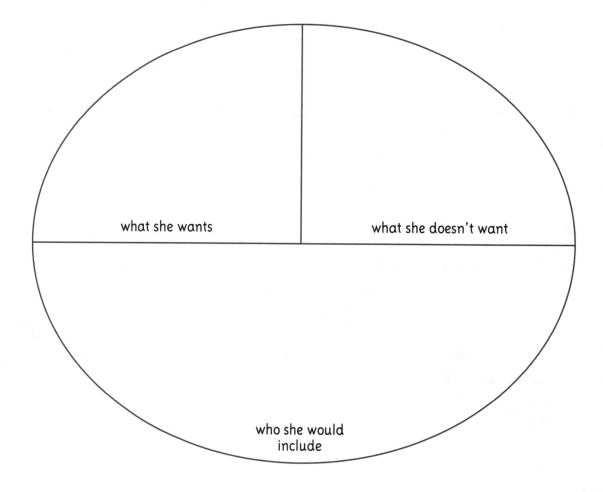

"The Red Gloves"
Siv Cedering

Hey, you forgot us!
Hurry back.

You will find one of us
behind the baseball diamond,
the other one
by the swing.

Without your hands,
we are five-room houses
waiting for our inhabitants
to come home.

We are soft shells
that miss
the snails that would give them
their own slow
speed.

[stanza break]

We are red wings
that have forgotten
how to fly.

When you find us,
put us on,

for like puppies who warm each other
all night
you will warm us
and we will warm
your hands

which must be
lost
valentines
without their red
envelopes.

"The Red Gloves"
Siv Cedering

The art of writing poetry is the art of creating images for the reader's mind. One of the best ways to create an image is to make comparisons that help the reader see, hear, and feel that image. The poet chooses words that capture sensory impressions. Rhythm may help to create an image, too. In "The Red Gloves," Siv Cedering uses these elements, as well as some wonderful metaphors and similes.

OPENERS Before reading the poem, ask students:

1. Think of one material thing that you have lost. Can you imagine what that thing might feel without you? What might it say to you?

2. Can you think of some thing in your life that wished it could speak to you? Your pet, for example, or your bike or favorite stuffed animal.

• Distribute Response Sheet 5 on page 61 and ask students to review the "As You Read" section.

• Distribute the poem and have students read it silently and then in pairs or small groups. Pick at least two volunteers to read the poem to the entire class.

• Have students complete the "After You Read" section of Response Sheet 5.

• Explore the poem with your class by focusing on:

FORM

"The Red Gloves" is a persona poem, which some people call a mask poem because the poet, in a sense, writes as if she were disguised as the subject of the poem. Cedering writes this poem as if she were a pair of lost red gloves. Tell your students that writing a mask poem is like wearing a costume at Halloween: We do it to become another person or thing. When I read this persona poem, it's as if the gloves are talking to me. After the students have had a little experience with this kind of poem, give them a chance to let their imaginations loose and write persona poems of their own. (See page 60 for other persona poems to share.)

STRUCTURE

The eight stanzas of the poem seem to be divided into three parts. In the first two stanzas, the gloves cry out to us, reminding us that we have left them behind at the playground. The middle part contains three stanzas that describe what the gloves are like without our hands in them. In the final three stanzas, the gloves tell us what it will be like when they are back on our hands. When you discuss the structure of the poem with your students, ask them if they can see the logical progression in the poem: losing the gloves, being without the gloves, finding the gloves. Remind them that part of this progression, and a very important part of every poem, is the end. A poem should sound finished. Cedering ends her poem with a strong image of "lost/valentines/without their red/envelopes/."

IMAGE

Poets create images by including words that appeal to the senses. So, even though we tend to think of "image" as relating to sight, an image in a poem will likely relate to other senses as well. For example, in the seventh stanza, Cedering uses the sense of touch to create an image:

> ...like puppies who warm each other
> all night
> you will warm us
> and we will warm
> your hands

We can all picture puppies, so Cedering uses that image to emphasize the warmth that the gloves will provide.

FIGURATIVE LANGUAGE

HAND OUT REPRODUCIBLE 5 One of the ways that poets create images is through figurative language such as the metaphors and similes that Cedering includes in stanzas three, four, and five. To help your students get a better understanding of how figurative language creates images, give them Reproducible 5 on page 62, ask them to read stanzas three, four, and five, and see if they can identify the similes and metaphors. In other words, to what does she compare the empty gloves?

After they have written their answers on the reproducible, discuss the essence of the comparison. For a metaphor or simile to work, the comparison must be clear, but not always upon a first reading. In stanza three, for example, Cedering compares the gloves to "five-room houses/waiting for our inhabitants/to come home." In the next stanza, the empty gloves are "soft shells/that miss/the snails." And in the fifth stanza of the poem, Cedering compares the limp gloves to "red wings/that have forgotten/how to fly." Each of these metaphors works well, but the connection to the gloves may not be immediately apparent.

When you have finished discussing the metaphors in the middle of the poem, ask your students if they can see the comparisons in the final stanza of the poem. I've already discussed the simile in stanza seven—"like puppies who warm each other"—but your students should be able to see the "lost/valentines" metaphor in the final stanza.

SOUND

If your students have read this poem aloud, they may have noticed some of the neat things that Cedering does with the sound of words. For example, she uses alliteration by starting the first three lines of stanza three with a word that starts with *w: Without, we, waiting.* And, if you look at the next stanza, you see how she piles up the *s* sound: "soft shells/that miss/the snails." And then she closes the stanza with "slow/speed." In the next to the last stanza, she uses *warm* as part of a phrase that serves as something of a refrain: "who warms," "will warm," and "will warm" again. Finally, she ends the poem with the *eh* sound in "red/envelopes." Don't forget, such techniques are best appreciated when the poem is read aloud.

RELATED POEMS

"Shell," Deborah Chandra
"Being a Kite," Jacqueline Sweeney
"Washing Machine," Bobbi Katz

Focus on the Poet

Siv Cedering, whose first name rhymes with "Steve," was born in Sweden but immigrated to this country when she was 14. She has written more than 2o books of poetry and fiction for adults and children, but she also is a translator, composer, and visual artist. One of her more popular children's books is *The Blue Horse and Other Night Poems* (Seabury Press,1978), for which she also did the illustrations. Her latest book of poems for adults is *Letters From an Observatory: New and Selected Poems, 1973–1998* (Karma Dog Editions). Prior to that, she published *Letters From The Floating World: New and Selected Poems* (University of Pittsburgh Press, 1984).

Name: _____ Date: _____

"The Red Gloves"
Siv Cedering

AS YOU READ

Look for any comparisons that Cedering makes.

AFTER YOU READ

Answer these questions:

1. What did you notice about "The Red Gloves"? Mark up the poem with underlines, circles, and arrows to show what you noticed.

2. Do you have any questions about the poem? Jot them down.

_____

_____

_____

_____

Poetic Terms

Here are some terms that will help you talk about the poem:

persona poem/mask poem: a poem in which the poet writes from the point of view of another person or thing

image: a picture the poet creates with vivid words that appeal to the reader's senses

metaphor: a comparison of two dissimilar things that implies some sort of equality between the things

simile: a comparison using "like" or "as"

alliteration: repetition of initial consonant sounds

Name: _____   Date: _____

"The Red Gloves"
Siv Cedering

After carefully reading the poem, record some of the metaphors and similes you found in the glove below.

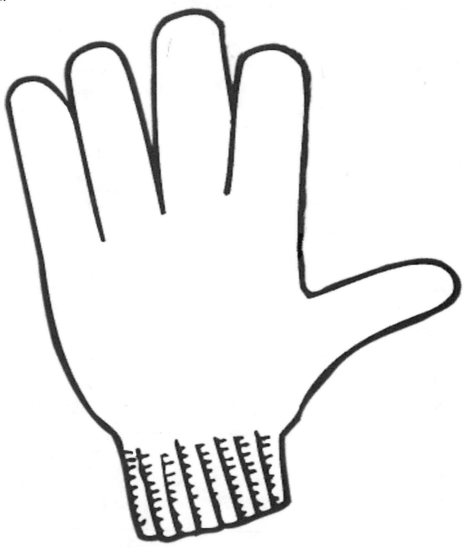

Opening a Door • Scholastic Professional Books

"The Telling Tree"
Linda Peavy

"I'll race you to the telling tree,"
she called past clang of recess bell,
then sped to be the first of three
to claim the oak whose tangled roots,
sprawled angular as spiders' legs,
were shelter enough for secret things.
Shedding thin coats, they dropped onto
the hard-packed clay, legs out,
back leaned against worn trunk,
coats snugged across them, blanket-like,
till yellow-brown plaid, dark navy, and red
were spread from root to rough, gnarled root
against the late November chill.
With only their faces out and free
there at the base of the telling tree
they shared the things they could not share
anywhere except that place.
Fran's mother was having a baby again.
Lee's dad had beaten her till she screamed.
Norma Jean's brother was back in jail.
And everyone knew that Freddy would fail
third grade and have to repeat next year.

And maybe you didn't go straight to hell
if your teeth touch the host—
but maybe you did,
and for other things, too. On and on
the secrets flew—nobody caring if anyone knew
all that they had to say to be free
there in the roots of the telling tree.

"The Telling Tree"
Linda Peavy

"The Telling Tree" engages many students because it tells a story of a friendship that is grounded in a special place. Peavy uses clear sensory details to describe both the place and the friendships. It provides further evidence that a poem need not be about the spectacular to be engaging. Peavy celebrates life through the "little things" she notices.

OPENERS Before reading the poem, ask students:

1. Do you have some secrets that you'll only tell your very best friends?

2. Think of a special place where you and your friends often hang out. How did you choose that spot?

• Distribute Response Sheet 6 on page 67 and ask students to review the "As You Read" section.

• Distribute the poem and have students read it silently and then in pairs or small groups. Pick at least two volunteers to read the poem to the entire class.

• Have students complete the "After You Read" section of Response Sheet 6.

• Explore the poem with your class by focusing on:

IMAGE

As I've noted before, poets create images with details that appeal to the senses. Sensory details make the image come alive for the reader. It's important for students to remember that a good poet uses all the senses to create an image. Not all the senses in every poem, of course, but just those that help create an image.

HAND OUT REPRODUCIBLE 6 Give students Reproducible 6 on page 68, ask them to read through the poem again, and jot down in the left column of Part I the specific details Peavy uses in the poems. In the right column, have them note to which sense the detail appeals. For example:

DETAIL   SENSE
clang of recess bell   hearing
tangled roots   sight

shedding thin coats	sight, touch
hard-packed clay	touch
coats snuggled across them	touch
late November chill	touch

Details like these clarify her images. Note how the poem would have been fuzzier if she had said "dirt" instead of "hard-packed clay"; "ring of recess bell" instead of "clang of recess bell"; and "coats covering them" instead of "coats snuggled across them."

In the second part of the poem, after the girls get to the telling tree, Peavy uses other details that are not as sensory as the ones at the beginning. Nonetheless, they contribute greatly to her image of the friends. Part II of Reproducible 6 gives your students a chance to zero in on these details, by identifying what the friends confess at the telling tree:

> Fran's mother was having a baby again.
>
> Lee's dad had beaten her till she screamed.
>
> Norma Jean's brother was back in jail.

WORD CHOICE

If your students look carefully at the three lines below, they may notice how Peavy adds a qualifying word or phrase to each one, which I've boldfaced below, to emphasize why these confessions are out of the ordinary, why they are so worth sharing:

> Fran's mother was having a baby **again**.
>
> Lee's dad had beaten her **till she screamed**.
>
> Norma Jean's brother was **back** in jail.

Although the qualifying words may seem insignificant, they reveal troubling patterns that are part of these children's lives: a mom having a baby again; a dad not only beating his child, but beating her "till she screamed"; and a brother who has returned to jail. By adding these five words to three lines in the poem, Peavy speaks volumes about the situations of these three young friends and shows us why the telling tree is so important:

> there at the base of the telling tree
>
> they shared the things they could not share
>
> anywhere except that place

Some of your more astute students might also notice other places where Peavy's word choice reveals deeper layers. For example, the girls race to the tree, "Shedding thin coats," just as they are anxious to shed some of their family secrets. She also uses the word "free" in two different ways in the poem. In line 14: "With only their faces out and free," gives their faces a physical freedom, but in the next to the last line, "free" is used in a more spiritual way: "the secrets flew—nobody caring if anyone knew/all that they had to say to be free."

STRUCTURE

The overall structure of the poem is quite simple: Three friends run outside during recess, hurry to the telling tree and get comfortable, and share family secrets. However, she includes the title three times in the poem: in the first line—"'I'll race you to the telling tree'"—and in the final line as well—"there in the roots of the telling tree"—using the phrase acts as bookends to, in a sense, hold the poem together. To make sure that this phrase is firmly in our minds, she also uses it in line 15—"there at the base of the telling tree"—where it acts as a connector between the opening of the poem and the closing.

RELATED POEMS

"I Still Have Everything You Gave Me," Naomi Shihab Nye
"Summertime Sharing," Nikki Grimes
"Muscling Rocks," Robert Morgan

Focus on the Poet

Linda Peavy was born in Mississippi, where she studied at Mississippi College and did graduate work at University of North Carolina at Chapel Hill. After teaching high school and college English for 10 years, she began working as a freelance writer.

Peavy has published short stories, poems, and nonfiction articles in many magazines and journals. Although she has yet to publish a book of her own poetry, her work is in a number of anthologies. She and Ursula Smith are senior historical consultants for the PBS miniseries "Frontier House." You can find more specific information about her life and work online at <www.olemiss.edu/mwp/dir/peavy_linda/index.html>.

Name: _____ Date: _____

"The Telling Tree"
Linda Peavy

AS YOU READ

1. Be on the lookout for details that come to you through your senses.

2. **Words to Know:** Here are some words that are important in the poem.

   angular: at an angle

   shedding: becoming free of

AFTER YOU READ

Answer these questions:

1. What did you notice about "The Telling Tree"? Mark up the poem with underlines, circles, and arrows to show what you noticed.

2. Do you have any questions about the poem? Jot them down.

_____

_____

_____

_____

Poetic Term

Here is a term that will help you talk about the poem:

image: a picture the poet creates with vivid words that appeal to the reader's senses.

Name: _____ Date: _____

"The Telling Tree"
Linda Peavy

PART I

After carefully reading "The Telling Tree," record some details that you noticed in the poem. Next to each detail, note which sense that detail appeals to.

DETAILS	SENSES

PART II

What secret does each girl share with her friends? Write them in the diagram below:

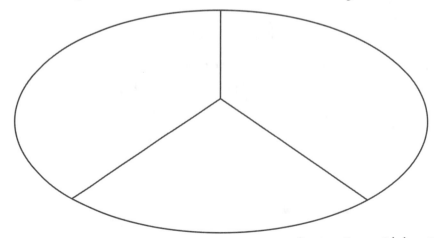

EXPLORATION 7

"A Room in the Past"
Ted Kooser

It's a kitchen. Its curtains fill

with a morning light so bright

you can't see beyond its windows

into the afternoon. A kitchen

falling through time with its things

in their places, the dishes jingling

up in the cupboard, the bucket

of drinking water rippled as if

a truck had just gone past, but that truck

was thirty years. No one's at home

in this room. Its counter is wiped,

and the dishrag hangs from its nail,

a dry leaf. In housedresses of mist,

blue aprons of rain, my grandmother

moved through this life like a ghost,

and when she had finished her years,

she put them all back in their places

and wiped out the sink, turning her back

on the rest of us, forever.

Scholastic Professional Books • Opening a Door

69

"A Room in the Past"
Ted Kooser

We often associate the people in our lives with a particular place. For example, I can still see my father repairing television sets in his basement workshop in the house where I grew up. It looked like the set of a grade-B science fiction movie. My older brother is forever fixed in my mind, hunched over a carburetor he was rebuilding in the garage, his fingers black with grease, a cigarette dangling from the corner of his mouth. In "A Room in the Past," Ted Kooser remembers his grandmother by making clear connections between her and the kitchen where she spent so many of her days.

OPENERS Before reading the poem, ask students:

1. When you think of one of your grandparents (or one of your aunts, uncles, or parents), what place do you associate with that person?

2. Think about your space at home—your room or the part of a room that you share with a sibling. What does your space say about you?

• Distribute Reproducible 7 on page 74 and ask students what their grandmothers are/were like. After a brief discussion, have them to fill in the columns in Part I with information about a grandparent or other significant person in their life. (The person they choose is less important than what they notice about her or him. The goal is for them see how character can be defined by concrete actions or objects.) The left column asks them to list four or five characteristics about that person. The right column asks them to write a detail—such as an action, a mannerism, an object—that supports each characteristic. For example, a student might say that her grandmother likes to cook and support that opinion with details such as:
  • her wide array of cookbooks
  • a small file box bursting with clipped and handwritten recipes
  • there always seems to be something simmering on the stove
  • the kitchen always smells delicious
  • she constantly invites visitors to "try this!"
• Distribute the poem and have students read it silently and then in pairs or small groups.

Pick at least two volunteers to read the poem to the entire class.

- Explore the poem with your class by focusing on:

CHARACTER

Although we never met Kooser's grandmother, the poet gives us a clear indication of what she was like. He gives no details about her appearance, but he does tell us about the kind of woman she was. A good poem suggests, and this poem suggests a great deal about the woman.

When your students have finished Part I of Reproducible 7, ask them to complete Part II, which asks them to do what they did in Part I, except, this time, look for information in the poem.

Although Kooser doesn't tell us everything about the woman, we come away with a clear sense that she likes order. Note the details that support this: "things in their places," "the dishes… in the cupboard," the "counter is wiped," and "the dish rag hangs from its nail." He goes beyond those details with lines 16 to 18:

> and when she had finished her years,
> she put them all back in their places
> and wiped out the sink…

Ask your students to go beyond their initial impressions of the grandmother. Can they see that she wasn't particularly warm or "grandmotherly"? After all, she "moved through this life like a ghost." And when her life was drawing to a close, she put things in order and "wiped out the sink, turning her back/on the rest of us, forever."

- Distribute Response Sheet 7 on page 73. Ask students to answer the questions and review the poetic terms. Continue exploring the poem by focusing on:

FIGURATIVE LANGUAGE

Coming across a good metaphor or simile in a poem is like making a wonderful discovery. Although "A Room in the Past" isn't filled with figurative language, it contains a few gems. The dishrag, for example, "hangs from its nail,/a dry leaf." Does that metaphor give your students a vivid picture? In line 15, Kooser writes that his grandmother "moved through this life like a ghost." What images does this simile conjure up for your students? In addition, he writes that the woman moved in "housedresses of mist,/blue aprons of rain."

SOUND

There's no end rhyme in this free verse poem, with the exception of "light so bright" in line two. Nonetheless, Kooser has a good ear for the sounds that words make, especially when they are in the company of other words. You can point out the repetition of the vowel sound, or assonance, in line three: "see beyond." Can they hear the *ee* sound in those words? They might notice the repetition of the *th* sound in lines five and six: "falling through time with its things/in their places."

Reading the poem aloud may make your students aware of the repetition of the short *i* sound throughout the poem. For example, Kooser uses the word *its* twice in the first line and four other times later. The short *i* sound is also heard in words like *with, in, if, this, finished.*

Don't worry if your students cannot pick out sounds like these right away. It takes some young readers time to get the hang of it, which is another reason for reading poems aloud as often as possible.

THE ENDING

In the last four lines, Kooser brings the poem to a slow and satisfying conclusion. Line 16—"and when she had finished her years"—gives us a clue that the end is approaching. But it's the final line and a half, especially the last word, that firmly closes the poem: "turning her back/on the rest of us, forever."

RELATED POEMS

"Grandfather's Heaven," Naomi Shihab Nye

"Granny," Ashley Bryan

"Ghost Story," Kathryn Stripling Byer

Focus on the Poet

Ted Kooser is one of my favorite poets. That's why I've included so many of his poems in my anthologies. Although he has never written a "children's" poem, his work is accessible to many young adult readers. He's published nine books of poetry, including three from the University of Pittsburgh Press: *Sure Signs* (1980), *One World at a Time* (1985), and *Weather Central* (1994). His most recent collection is *Winter Morning Walks: One Hundred Postcards to Jim Harrison* (Carnegie-Mellon University Press, 2001). In addition, his poems have appeared in many literary journals and magazines.

If you go to <theatlantic.com/unbound/poetry> and search on "Kooser," you can hear the author read his poems.

Name: _____ Date: _____

"A Room in the Past"
Ted Kooser

1. What did you notice about "A Room in the Past"? Mark up the poem with underlines, circles, and arrows to show what you noticed.

2. Do you have any questions about the poem? Jot them down.

_____

_____

_____

3. How would you describe the woman that Kooser writes about in his poem?

_____

_____

_____

Poetic Terms

Here are some terms that will help you talk about the poem:

figurative language: non-literal expressions to get across certain ideas or things more vividly

metaphor: a direct comparison of two dissimilar things that implies some sort of equality between the things

simile: a comparison using "like" or "as"

end rhyme: similar sounding words at the ends of lines

free verse: poetry that is free of regular rhythm or rhyme

assonance: repetition of vowel sounds in words

Name: _____   Date: _____

"A Room in the Past"
Ted Kooser

PART I

Take a few minutes to think about one of your grandparents or another person you know quite well, such as one of your parents. In the left column write a few characteristics of that person, for example, *kind*. In the right column write a detail or two that suggests or demonstrates that trait, for example, *my grandmother was always taking in stray cats.*

CHARACTERISTICS	DETAILS

PART II

In the columns below, record your impressions of the grandmother in "A Room in the Past." In the left column, write down a few characteristics of this woman, and in the other column write a few details from the poem that demonstrate or suggest that trait.

CHARACTERISTICS	DETAILS

"The Bells"
Edgar Allan Poe

1

Hear the sledges with the bells—
Silver bells!
What a world of merriment their melody foretells!
How they tinkle, tinkle, tinkle,
In the icy air of night!
While the stars that oversprinkle
All the Heavens, seem to twinkle
With a crystalline delight;
Keeping time, time, time,
In a sort of Runic rhyme,
To the tintinnabulation that so musically wells
From the bells, bells, bells, bells,
Bells, bells, bells—
From the jingling and the tinkling of the bells.

2

Hear the mellow wedding bells—
Golden bells!
What a world of happiness their harmony foretells!
Through the balmy air of night
How they ring out their delight!—
From the molten-golden notes
And all in tune,
What a liquid ditty floats
To the turtle-dove that listens while she gloats
On the moon!
Oh, from out the sounding cells
What a gush of euphony voluminously wells!
How it swells!
How it dwells
On the Future!—how it tells
Of the rapture that impels
To the swinging and the ringing
Of the bells, bells, bells!—
Of the bells, bells, bells, bells,
Bells, bells, bells—
To the rhyming and the chiming of the bells!

3

Hear the loud alarum bells—
Brazen bells!
What tale of terror, now, their turbulency tells!
In the startled ear of Night
How they scream out their affright!
Too much horrified to speak,
They can only shriek, shriek,
Out of tune,
In a clamorous appealing to the mercy of the fire—
In a mad expostulation with the deaf and frantic fire,
Leaping higher, higher, higher,
With a desperate desire
And a resolute endeavor
Now—now to sit, or never,
By the side of the pale-faced moon.
Oh, the bells, bells, bells,
What a tale their terror tells
Of despair!
How they clang and clash and roar!
What a horror they outpour
In the bosom of the palpitating air!
Yet the ear, it fully knows,
By the twanging
And the clanging,
How the danger ebbs and flows:—
Yes, the ear distinctly tells
In the jangling
And the wrangling,
How the danger sinks and swells,
By the sinking or the swelling in the anger of the bells—
Of the bells—
Of the bells, bells, bells, bells,
Bells, bells, bells—
In the clamor and the clangor of the bells.

4

Hear the tolling of the bells—
Iron bells!
What a world of solemn thought their monody compels!
In the silence of the night
How we shiver with affright

At the melancholy meaning of the tone!
For every sound that floats
From the rust within their throats
Is a groan.
And the people—ah, the people
They that dwell up in the steeple
All alone,
And who, tolling, tolling, tolling,
In that muffled monotone,
Feel a glory in so rolling
On the human heart a stone—
They are neither man nor woman—
They are neither brute nor human,
They are Ghouls:—
And their king it is who tolls:—
And he rolls, rolls, rolls, rolls
A Paean from the bells!
And his merry bosom swells
With the Paean of the bells!
And he dances and he yells;
Keeping time, time, time,
In a sort of Runic rhyme,
To the Paean of the bells—
Of the bells: —
Keeping time, time, time,
In a sort of Runic rhyme,
To the throbbing of the bells—
Of the bells, bells, bells—
To the sobbing of the bells:—
Keeping time, time, time,
As he knells, knells, knells,
In a happy Runic rhyme,
To the rolling of the bells—
Of the bells, bells, bells:—
To the tolling of the bells—
Of the bells, bells, bells, bells,
Bells, bells, bells—
To the moaning and the groaning of the bells.

"The Bells"
Edgar Allan Poe

Known primarily as a writer of dark short stories, Edgar Allan Poe was also quite a popular poet in his short life. Although many of his poems are spooky and sinister, such as "The Raven," he also wrote poems of lost innocence and lost love, such as "Annabel Lee" and "To Helen." His poems are rich with rhythm and, like "The Bells," come alive when they are read aloud. This poem may surprise your students who only know Poe as the master of the macabre.

OPENERS Before reading the poem, ask students:

1. What do you know about poems by Edgar Allan Poe? Do you expect a certain kind of poem? A poem about a certain subject?

2. In your notebook, make two short lists. On one list, write three or four words that you think are harsh sounding, for example, *crash, wreck,* and *yell.* Then write another list of three or four words that are soft sounding, for example, *silk, fog,* and *whisper.*

- Distribute Response Sheet 8 on page 81 and ask students to review the "words to know" in the "As You Read" section. Despite Poe's popularity in middle school classrooms, he presents a challenge to many readers who stumble over his archaic vocabulary. Some of your students will be able to read "The Bells" with minimal trouble. Others won't. So it's a good idea to let students know that they will face many challenging words in this long poem and supply the response sheet with some of the more troublesome words defined: *sledges, Runic, tintinnabulation, ditty, voluminously, turbulency, clamorous, expostulation, palpitating, twanging, monody, melancholy, monotone, Ghouls, Paean.* Be sure to have dictionaries available, too, for other words students may find challenging.

- Distribute the poem and have students read it silently and then in pairs or small groups. Pick at least two volunteers to read the poem to the entire class.

- Have students complete the "After You Read" section of Response Sheet 8.

- Explore the poem with your class by focusing on:

CHORAL READING

Because this is a "sound poem" in so many ways, it demands to be read aloud as a choral perform-ance. Divide your class into four groups, one for each stanza, and arrange the kids according to their voices. Those with the highest voices (or with voices that can function in the higher range) should read stanza one which is filled with merriment and melody of the silver bells. Those with the lowest voices (or with voices that can function in the lower range) should read stanza four, which is filled with solemn, melancholy iron bells. Finally, have students with appropriate voices reading stanza two, with its "mellow wedding… Golden bells," and stanza three, with its "loud alarum… Brazen bells."

It may take a little doing to find the right voices for each stanza, but it will be worth the time. The only way that poetry readers can actually hear the music of a poem is to listen to it read aloud. And, with practice, your students will capture the different music in each section of "The Bells."

SOUND

Poe is a master at using a variety of sound tools. In "The Bells," he creates several patterns. Note how each stanza begins with the same phrase, "Hear the [kind of bells]," for example:

> Hear the sledges with the bells—
>
> Silver bells!
>
> What a world of merriment their melody foretells!

The other stanzas begin with the same pattern.

Ask students if they can find phrases that Poe repeats. They may notice phrases such as, "How they tinkle, tinkle, tinkle" and "Keeping time, time, time" in stanza one. And what he repeats in the final stanza: "And who, tolling, tolling, tolling" as well as "And he rolls, rolls, rolls." This sort of repetition appears throughout the poem.

Notice, too, how Poe repeats the word "bells" throughout the poem. It is itself a musical word, so repeating it carries that music from beginning to end of the poem. In fact, he repeats the word 8 to 13 times in the final five or six lines of each stanza. It's also the last word of the poem.

Ask your students to look for other patterns in the poem. For example, they might notice that, although Poe maintains no formal rhyme scheme (a recurring pattern of end rhyme) throughout the poem the first five lines mostly follow a scheme of *aaabb*. And, in all stanzas, "bells" appears at the end of at least three lines.

Another pattern, of sorts, is the way Poe uses words that capture the sounds of the various kinds of bells. For example, notice how lines 3 to 8 of the first stanza convey the sound of the silver bells:

> What a world of merriment their melody foretells!
> How the tinkle, tinkle, tinkle,
> > In the icy air of night!
> While the stars that oversprinkle
> All the Heavens, seem to twinkle
> > With a crystalline delight

HAND OUT REPRODUCIBLE 8 Ask your choral groups to look carefully at the stanza they read and look for words and phrases that reflect the sound of the bells. Then have the whole class fill out Reproducible 8 on page 82 and discuss what it finds.

If you have discussed sound devices such as alliteration and assonance, ask students to find examples of where Poe used those devices in the poem. They should notice phrases like "merriment their melody," "Runic rhyme," "happiness their harmony," and "frantic fire," to name a few.

RELATED POEMS

Lyrical poems by Poe:
"Annabel Lee"
"To Helen"

Eerie poems by Poe:
"The Raven"
"Lenore"

Focus on the Poet

Your students may know something of the short (1809–1849) and difficult life of Edgar Allan Poe. Despite living only 40 years, he was able to shine in a number of literary endeavors, including poetry, fiction, and critical essays. He is, in fact, considered by some to be the father of the modern detective story because of his short story "The Murders in the Rue Morgue" (1841).

Two of the better Poe web sites are <www.eapoe.org>, which is maintained by the Edgar Allan Poe Society of Baltimore, and <www.poemuseum.org>, the site of the Poe Museum.

Name: _____   Date: _____

"The Bells" Edgar Allan Poe

AS YOU READ

Words to Know: Here are some words that are important in the poem.

sledges: a long heavy hammer; *Runic:* referring to any of several alphabets used by Germanic people from the 3rd to the 13th century; *tintinnabulation:* ringing; *turbulency:* violently agitated or disturbed; *clamorous:* a loud outcry; *expostulations:* trying to convince someone; *palpitating:* to tremble, shake, or quiver; *monody:* an ode or elegy; *Ghouls:* grave robbers or creatures who delight in the revolting or morbid; *Paean:* a song of joyful praise

AFTER YOU READ

1. What did you notice about "The Bells"? Mark up the poem with underlines, circles, and arrows to show what you noticed.

2. Do you have any questions about the poem? Jot them down.

_____

_____

3. Reread two of the stanzas and see if you can find words that sound like the bells of those stanzas.

_____

_____

Poetic Terms

Here are some terms that will help you enjoy this poem:

stanza: a group of lines in poetry, usually similar in length and pattern

rhyme scheme: the pattern of end rhymes in a poem

alliteration: repetition of initial consonant sound in words

assonance: repetition of vowel sounds in words

Name: _____   Date: _____

"The Bells"
Edgar Allan Poe

In the spaces below, list words and phrases that describe the bells in the opening lines of each stanza.

Silver Bells	Golden Bells
Brazen Bells	**Iron Bells**

"Famous"

Naomi Shihab Nye

The river is famous to the fish.

The loud voice is famous to silence,
which knew it would inherit the earth
before anybody said so.

The cat sleeping on the fence is famous to the birds
watching him from the birdhouse.

The tear is famous, briefly, to the cheek.

The idea you carry close to your bosom
is famous to your bosom.

The boot is famous to the earth,
more famous than the dress shoe,
which is famous only to floors.

The bent photograph is famous to the one who carries it
and not at all famous to the one who is pictured.

I want to be famous to shuffling men
who smile while crossing streets,
sticky children in grocery lines,
famous as the one who smiled back.

I want to be famous in the way a pulley is famous,
or a buttonhole, not because it did anything spectacular,
but because it never forgot what it could do.

"Famous"
Naomi Shihab Nye

"Famous" is a gentle poem that turns the notion of being "famous" on its head. While many people equate "famous" with limousines, glitz, and stacks of cash, Nye sees it is as being much quieter than that, much closer to the heart. She tell us, for example, "The tear is famous, briefly, to the cheek." Writing something of a list poem, Nye chooses common, specific things to show us how she sees the notion of "famous."

OPENERS Before reading the poem, ask students:

1. What does "famous" mean to you?

2. Name some things or people or places that you consider to be "famous."

• Distribute the poem and have students read it silently and then in pairs or small groups. Pick at least two volunteers to read the poem to the entire class.

• Distribute the Response Sheet 9 on page 87. Ask students to answer the questions and review the poetic terms.

• Explore the poem with your class by focusing on:

STRUCTURE

Nye's free verse poem follows a simple pattern: each stanza contains a clear example or two of something she sees as famous, from beginning—"The river is famous to the fish"—to end:

> I want to be famous in the way a pulley is famous,
>
> or a buttonhole, not because it did anything spectacular,
>
> but because it never forgot what it could do.

HAND OUT REPRODUCIBLE **9** If you want to emphasize this structure, have nine students each read aloud one stanza of the poem. Each voice will indicate an example of something "famous." From there, give students Reproducible 9 on page 88, which asks them to look carefully at each stanza and jot down a few words that explains how or why the object in the poem is famous. For example, in stanza three, the cat is famous to the birds because of the danger it represents.

DETAILS

After students have had time to consider each stanza and jot down notes, let them discuss the famous things that Nye has chosen. Can they see any commonalities among those things? They are all everyday things: a river, a cat, a tear, a boot, a bent photograph.

It's important for students to see how Nye takes an everyday thing, but looks at it in an unexpected way to illustrate her notion of "famous." The bent photograph, for example, isn't famous to the person in the picture. Rather, it is famous to "the one who carries it." Note, too, that the photograph is bent, suggesting that it's been carried around for a while. By looking at things in an original way, she adds delicious surprises to her poem. No wonder she wants "to be famous in the way a pulley is famous," not because it can help lift heavy objects, but "because it never forgot what it could do." I suspect Walt Whitman might consider her everyday things to be miracles. (See his poem on page 101.)

WORD CHOICE

Nye's words not only give a vivid picture, but also have a gentleness about them. Notice some of her choices: a sleeping cat, a tear, a bent photograph, a smile, sticky children, buttonhole. They are all gentle and quiet. Ask your students how the poem would have been different if she had chosen phrases such as:

- a guard dog is famous to the derelict cars it defends
- the bullet is famous to the rifle
- the sword is famous to the hand of a warrior
- a scream is famous to the roller coaster

So, the poet not only selects words that show a different side of "famous," but also unites them with a quality of gentleness.

SOUND

Nye uses the word *famous* throughout the poem, sometimes two or three times in a stanza, not only to remind us of what the poem is about, but also to hold the poem together. She uses alliteration, particularly with the *f* sound of famous. In line one, for example, she writes "famous to the fish." In the last line of the sixth stanza, she writes, "famous only to floors." Stanza eight contains assonance with the repetition of the long *i* sound, as in *smile while,* as well as in *lines* and *smiled.*

Her first seven stanzas begin in the same way, with *The* followed by a noun, in most cases—for example, "The river," "The loud voice," "The cat," and "The tear." Also, the last two stanzas begin in the same way: "I want to be famous…" While such repetition may seem unimportant to your students, it gives the poem its rhythm. When you reach this point in your classroom discussion, you might have the students read the poem aloud again and see if they can recognize that repetition.

RELATED POEMS

"Fog," Marilyn Singer
"Mantel," Cynthia Rylant
"The Peace of Wild Things," Wendell Berry

Focus on the Poet

Naomi Shihab Nye was born in St. Louis to an American mother and a Palestinian father. Since publishing her first poem at seven years old, poetry has been an important part of her life. The list of books Nye has written and edited is long. She's published six books of her own poems, including *Fuel* (BOA Editions, 1998), *Red Suitcase* (BOA Editions, 1994), and *19 Varieties of Gazelle: Poems of the Middle East* (HarperCollins, 2002). Her poetry anthologies for young readers include *This Same Sky: A Collection of Poems from Around the World* (Simon and Schuster, 1996) and *The Space Between Our Footsteps: Poems and Paintings from the Middle East* (Simon and Schuster, 1998).

You can find a full list of her books at <voices.cla.umn.edu/authors/NaomiShihabNye.html>, which is a site for "Voices from the Gap, Women of Color." She is also included in the "Find a Poet" section of the Academy of American Poets <www.poets.org>. Nye lives in San Antonio.

Name: _____ Date: _____

"Famous"
Naomi Shihab Nye

1. What did you notice about "Famous"? Mark up the poem with underlines, circles, and arrows to show what you noticed.

2. Do you have any questions about the poem? Jot them down.

_____

_____

_____

3. Does your definition of "famous" differ from the poet's definition? Explain your opinion in a few words.

_____

_____

_____

Poetic Terms

Here are some terms that will help you talk about this poem:

stanza: a group of lines in poetry, usually similar in length and pattern

alliteration: repetition of initial consonant sound in words

assonance: repetition of vowel sounds in words

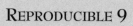

Name: _____   Date: _____

"Famous"
Naomi Shihab Nye

After carefully reading the poem, find six things that the poet considers "famous." List each one in the boxes below and explain how and why it is famous and to what or who it is famous. For example, the "cat sleeping on the fence" is famous to the birds because it's dangerous.

"Wintered Sunflowers"

Richard Snyder

Like rusted shower-heads at beach resorts,

and nearly as forlorn;

or as if some heavy-handed human

grief had bent them so to mourn

the winter they've come through.

Their only tropism now toward their own

pale shadows on the blue

and frosted ground. The birds have picked their brains

to husked remains and plagiarized

their black eyes. They've snowed their gold

to Ikhnaton and stand

tracking stations with nothing to behold.

EXPLORATION 10

"Wintered Sunflowers"
Richard Snyder

How wonderfully Richard Snyder can describe dead sunflowers. In 12 lines, he makes all kinds of comparisons to help them come alive for the reader. In spots he gives the flowers human qualities. He includes a couple of nifty word plays and he even throws in some rhyme. The end of the poem will most likely stump your students initially, but I hope my commentaries provide ideas to guide them through it. With your help, your students will come to see "Wintered Sunflowers" as a poem that requires a little more work than some, yet is worth the effort.

OPENERS   Before reading the poem, ask students:

1. When you observe the world, what sorts of things are you most apt to notice?
2. What are some comparisons you have made between things you've noticed in the world?

- Distribute Response Sheet 10 on page 93 and ask students to review the "words to know" in the "As You Read" section.
- Distribute the poem and have students read it silently and then in pairs or small groups. Pick at least two volunteers to read the poem to the entire class.
- Have students complete the "After You Read" section of Response Sheet 10.
- Explore the poem with your class by focusing on:

WORD CHOICE

There are a number of words and references in "Wintered Sunflowers" that may give your students trouble when they read it. Students will most likely be able to figure out some words by looking closely at how they are used. Other words, however, they may need to find in the dictionary. Students are often reluctant to "look it up," but it is a necessary skill. As they read more sophisticated literature, they will encounter more words that are new to them, so I don't shy away from using poems that have some challenging vocabulary. Remind your students that the dictionary is a valuable tool that should always be close at hand.

You might begin your exploration by asking students to read the poem and underline words that they don't understand. They might underline: *forlorn, tropism, plagiarized, Ikhnaton.* Write the words on the board and ask students to try to figure out the meanings from the way they're used in the poem. They'll likely see that *forlorn* means alone, abandoned. By the time students reach middle school, they should know what *plagiarize* means. But even if they don't, the context of the poem will help them see that it means to steal. I had to look up *tropism* to find out its meaning: "the responsive growth of movement or an organism to or away from an external stimulus." In other words, how a flower or plant leans toward the sun. I had to dig even deeper to learn that *Ikhnaton* (also spelled *Akhnaton*) was a king of Egypt of the 18th dynasty (1353–36 BC), who established a monotheistic cult of Aton, a sun god. I would never expect middle school students to know this. I would provide a definition and let them explore how the word fits into the poem.

FIGURATIVE LANGUAGE

HAND OUT REPRODUCIBLE 10 This poem is woven together with comparisons, particularly personification, when the writer gives human qualities to inanimate objects. After your students have had the chance to read the poem aloud, give them Reproducible 10 on page 94 and ask them to note the comparisons in the poems. Make sure they understand that they must connect something in the poem to something outside the poem. For example, in lines 8 to 10 there is this example of personification: "The birds have picked their brains/to husked remains and plagiarized/their black eyes." The flowers, in a sense, are being compared to a human head that has been attacked by the birds, losing its "brains" and "black eyes."

Your students will no doubt notice other comparisons. Among them, how the sunflowers are like "rusted shower-heads at beach resorts." They are bent "as of some heavy-handed human/grief had bent them so to mourn." (Note the personification.) In lines 10 to 11 the flowers have "snowed their gold/to Ikhnaton." In other words, they have given up their golden petals to the sun god. In the final image in the poem, the flowers are "tracking stations with nothing to behold." The sunflowers no long follow the track of the sun. Winter and hungry birds have left them empty.

Comparisons like these work because we can see the connection the poet is making between something in the poem and something outside the poem. That connection leads us to understanding the essence of the poem's images.

SOUND

Although this is a free verse poem, Snyder sneaks in some rhyme. When your students read the poem aloud they may pick out some end rhymes such as *forlorn/mourn* and *gold/behold*. Have your students reread the middle of the poem where Snyder rhymes *brains* at the end of line eight with *remains*, the third word in the next line. He also rhymes plagiarized at the end of line nine with eyes, the third word in line 10.

By reading the poem aloud to your students, you can help them hear the rhythm of this poem. Point out the music in lines 3 to 5, as well as the alliteration in the first line:

> ...as if some heavy-handed human
>
> grief had bent them so to mourn
>
> the winter they've come through.

Lines 7 to 10 hold more music:

> ...The birds have picked their brains
>
> to husked remains and plagiarized
>
> their black eyes.

Just as some people have a hard time dancing because they cannot hear the rhythm of music, some of your students may not hear the rhythm of poetry. At least, not at first. Remember, some students need a lot of opportunities to hear poems read aloud before they will hear the rhythm of a poem. All the more reason for reading aloud to be a standard part of your curriculum.

RELATED POEMS

"Sunflower," John Updike

"Looking at Mushrooms," Constance Levy

"Poppies," Roy Scheele

Focus on the Poet

Richard Snyder (1925–1986) wrote poetry, fiction, and plays. He taught for a number of years in the English department of Ashland University in Ohio before serving as department chair for the last 15 years of his life. Co-founder of the Ashland Poetry Press, Snyder also began one of the first undergraduate creative writing majors in the country. His best poems can be found in *Practicing Our Sighs: The Collected Poems of Richard Snyder* (Ashland Poetry Press, 1989).

Name: _____ Date: _____

"Wintered Sunflowers"
Richard Snyder

AS YOU READ

Words to Know: Here are some words that are important to the poem.

forlorn: deserted or abandoned

tropism: the responsive growth of movement or an organism to or away from an external stimulus

plagiarized: to use and pass off as one's own the ideas or words of another

Ikhnaton: king of Egypt of the 18th dynasty (1353–36 BC), who established a monotheistic cult of Aton, a sun god.

AFTER YOU READ

Answer these questions:

1. What did you notice about "Wintered Sunflowers"? Mark up the poem with underlines, circles, and arrows to show what you noticed. Make sure you circle a couple of comparisons that appear in this poem.

2. Do you have any questions about the poem? Jot them down.

_____

_____

_____

Poetic Terms

Here are some terms that will help you talk about this poem:

personification: a comparison that gives human qualities to inanimate objects

end rhyme: similar sounding words at the ends of lines

alliteration: repetition of initial consonant sounds in words

Name: _____   Date: _____

"Wintered Sunflowers"
Richard Snyder

After carefully reading the poem, find a few comparisons. Then, in the ovals below, name the things being compared.

Snyder
compares ⬭ to ⬭

Snyder
compares ⬭ to ⬭

Snyder
compares ⬭ to ⬭

Opening a Door • Scholastic Professional Books

"Lullaby"
Steve Kowit (after Atila Josef)

Sweet love, everything
closes its eyes now to sleep.
The cat
       has stretched out
at the foot of your bed
& the little bug
          lays its head
in its arms
& your jacket
that's draped on the chair:
every button has fallen asleep,
even the poor torn cuff...
            & your flute
& your paper boat
& your candy bar
        snug in its wrapper.
Outside,
the evening is closing its eyes.
Even the hill to the dark
woods
has fallen asleep
on its side
       in a quilt of blue snow.

EXPLORATION 11

"Lullaby"
Steve Kowit

In her poem "Famous," which appears on page 83, Naomi Shihab Nye uses a number of gentle words to create a quiet mood. Steve Kowit uses a similar technique in "Lullaby," which makes sense given the definition of lullaby, a song sung to a child at bedtime. Kowit's details give us the image of a world going to sleep, inside the child's room and outside as well.

OPENERS Before reading the poem, ask students:

1. Do you have any rituals that you practice when you go to sleep? Any special activities that are part of your bedtime routine?

2. Do you remember anything special about bedtime when you were younger? For example, did someone read or sing to you?

- Distribute Response Sheet 11 on page 99 and ask students to review the "word to know" in the "As You Read" section.

- Distribute the poem and have students read it silently and then in pairs or small groups. Pick at least two volunteers to read the poem to the entire class. Readers may instinctively read the poem in a reverent, lullaby tone of voice. If they don't, suggest they do, given the nature of the poem. You might even experiment by having someone read it in an excessively loud voice, which should get a collective laugh when students notice that the volume does not fit the poem. Then have someone read it in a voice barely above a whisper. Do students notice the difference in how the poem feels when it was read in different ways? This experiment can serve as a reminder that, when you read a poem aloud, you need to practice it several times to find the appropriate way to convey it.

- Have students complete the "After You Read" section of Response Sheet 11.

- Explore the poem with your class by focusing on:

DETAILS

HAND OUT REPRODUCIBLE 11 Kowit's "Lullaby" is a list poem. To help your students notice that, have them work on Reproducible 11 on page 100, which asks them to notice the details that support the poet's assertion in the opening two lines that "everything/closes its eyes now to sleep." Specifically, students should be able to identify the things that are going to sleep and, when possible, show how they are going to sleep. They might notice the following:

Inside the house

1. cat	has stretched out at the foot of the bed
2. little bug	laid its head in its arms
3. jacket	draped on the chair, every button asleep
4. flute	
5. paper boat	
6. candy bar	snug in its wrapper

Outside the house

1. evening	closing its eyes
2. hill	fallen asleep on its side

Kowit attaches no verb to the flute and the paper boat, but does not need to since these toys are at rest. No one is playing the flute. The boat is not sailing in the water.

MOOD

As you and your students discuss the things in the poem that are closing their eyes "now for sleep," ask them to look carefully at the verbs that Kowit uses. Do they seem to have anything in common? Do your students notice that the verbs are restful, yet specific: *stretched out* (at the foot of the bed), *lays* (its head), *draped, snug* (in its wrapper), *closing* (its eyes), and *fallen asleep,* which is used twice. A skilled poet uses specific words or types of words to create an overall mood. Naomi Shihab Nye creates a gentle mood in "Famous." Kowit creates a hushed mood in "Lullaby."

STRUCTURE

After your students examine the verbs Kowit uses, they may be prepared to comment on the structure of the poem. In other words, how did Kowit build this poem? He starts by addressing the child in the first line, "Sweet love," and then he mentions things in the room that are going to sleep, a one-sentence list that goes on for 16 lines. At line 17 he switches his vision to mention a few things outside the child's room that are going to sleep, including two images that, the class may notice, are created with personification: "the evening is closing its eyes" and "the hill… has fallen asleep/on its side." Why is Kowit not content to confine his lullaby observations to the child's room? Who knows. Perhaps he wants to show the child that even the big things in the outside world, like hills, go to sleep in their own way.

Your students might notice that the poet has chosen to structure a poem with "bookends." He begins the poem by telling the child that "everything/closes its eyes now to sleep." And he returns to that notion at the close: "the evening is closing its eyes" and "the hill to the dark/woods/has fallen asleep."

RELATED POEMS

"Night Song," Eve Merriam

"Night Sounds," Felice Holman

"Mama, Mama, Catch Me a Star," Jane Yolen

> ## Focus on the Poet
>
> Steve Kowit is a California poet who has published his poems in many magazines and journals. His most recent collection of poems is *The Dumbell Nebula* (Heyday Books, 2000). He has also written *In the Palm of Your Hand: The Poet's Portable Workshop* (Tillbury House, 1995), a guide to writing poetry drawn from Kowit's 20 years of leading writing workshops.

Name: _____   Date: _____

"Lullaby"
Steve Kowit

AS YOU READ

Word to Know: Here's a word that is important in the poem.

draped: to cover or hang with

AFTER YOU READ

Answer these questions:

1. What did you notice about "Lullaby"? Mark up the poem with underlines, circles, and arrows to show what you noticed.

2. Do you have any questions about the poem? Jot them down.

_____

_____

_____

3. Did you notice a couple of things that are going to sleep in the poem?

_____

_____

_____

Poetic Terms

Here are some terms that will help you enjoy this poem:

personification: a comparison that gives human qualities to inanimate objects

mood: the atmosphere in a piece of writing

Name: _____   Date: _____

"Lullaby"
Steve Kowit

Kowit begins his poem by saying "everything/closes its eyes now to sleep." Find details in the poem that support that. Specifically, look for things that are going to sleep inside the house and outside the house. When possible, write down how they are going to sleep.

Inside the house   Outside the house

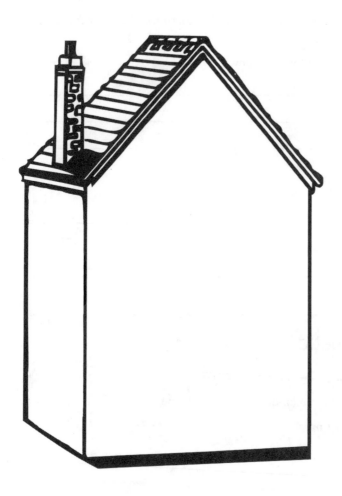

"Miracles"

Walt Whitman

Why, who makes much of a miracle?
As to me I know of nothing else but miracles,
Whether I walk the streets of Manhattan,
Or dart my sight over the roofs of houses toward the sky,
Or wade with naked feet along the beach just in the edge of
　　　　the water,
Or stand under trees in the woods,
Or talk by day with anyone I love, or sleep in the bed at night
　　　　with anyone I love,
Or sit at table at dinner with the rest,
Or look at strangers opposite me riding in the car,
Or watch honey-bees busy around the hive of a summer
　　　　forenoon,
Or animals feeding in the fields,
Or birds, or the wonderfulness of insects in the air,
Or the wonderfulness of the sundown, or of stars shining so
　　　　quiet and bright,
Or the exquisite delicate thin curve of the new moon in
　　　　spring;
These with the rest, one and all, are to me miracles,
The whole referring, yet each distinct and in its place.

To me every hour of the light and dark is a miracle,
Every cubic inch of space is a miracle,
Every square yard of the surface of the earth is spread with
　　　　the same,
Every foot of the interior swarms with the same.

To me the sea is a continual miracle,
The fishes that swim—the rocks—the motion of the
　　　　waves—
　　　　the ships with men in them,
What stranger miracles are there?

"Miracles"
Walt Whitman

If your students have had limited exposure to free verse poems, they may react to Walt Whitman's poems with confusion and aversion as did critics in the 19th century. Those critics preferred the rhyming poems of Longfellow, Whittier, Poe, and Bryant, not to mention the popular English Romantic poets such as Wordsworth and Keats. Nonetheless, Whitman gives your students a chance to experience all that he brought to poetry: gusto, the language of "everyperson," and a spirit as wide as the universe.

OPENERS Before reading the poem, ask students:

1. Think of some common, everyday thing—a "little" thing—that you are grateful for. What makes you feel grateful for it?
2. What do you consider a "miracle"? Have you had many miracles in your life?

- Distribute Response Sheet 12 on page 105 and ask students to review the "As You Read" section.
- Distribute the poem and have students read it silently and then in pairs or small groups. Pick at least two volunteers to read the poem to the entire class.
- Have students complete the "After You Read" section of Response Sheet 12.
- Explore the poem with your class by focusing on:

FORM

List poems have a long and respected pedigree. There are list poems in the Bible. Part of the *Iliad* is a list. John Milton and William Blake included lists in their poems. The Beat Poets wrote list poems. So did Pablo Neruda and Robinson Jeffers. Of all American poets, however, there is none more skilled at writing the list poem (or catalog poem, as some call it) than Walt Whitman. Many of the poems in *Leaves of Grass* are list poems. Whitman's list poems, like "Miracles," often capture his exuberance about living in a world of wonders.

Students must understand that a list poem is not merely a list. The list poem requires the hard work that makes any good poem come alive. It is Whitman's vivid language that makes "Miracles" a list poem, along with its sound, repetition, words, and deliberate structure.

SOUND

Walt Whitman's poems are great to read aloud because they sprawl along like a strong river. This poem is especially good to read aloud because its enthusiasm for life is so obvious. Whitman's wild embrace of life is contagious. In addition, some of the poetic devices that he uses in the poem add to its passion.

It's also important to have your students read this poem aloud because it sounds different from many of the others in this book. I suggest having a couple of students read the entire poem aloud. Then, to make things a little more interesting, ask for a volunteer to be the "narrator" of the poem. His or her job is to read the first three lines and lines 19 to 30. Each of the other lines should be read by a different student, which will yield a wonderfully varied effect. Conclude by having the whole class read the entire poem to capture the robust quality that Whitman heard in the world around him.

After the reading, ask the students what they noticed as they listened to the poem. Some of them may recognize how the long lines are smoother and more flowing than the short lines in other poems they may have read. Generally, this is the case: longer lines carry a smoother rhythm than shorter lines. To help your students understand this, read "Cottontail" on page 39 and see if they can hear the difference in the flow of each poem.

REPETITION

Part of the rhythm of the poem comes from the repetition. One kind of repetition that Whitman uses in "Miracles" is repetition of a specific word or phrase. For example, he uses the word "Or" to begin 11 lines of the poem. Later in the poem he begins three lines with "Every."

Another kind of repetition is a sort of structural repetition whereby the poet repeats a rhetorical structure. For example, if you look at the first seven lines that begin with "Or," you'll notice that each conjunction is followed by a one-syllable verb, as in "Or dart," "Or wade," "Or stand." The next four times he uses "Or" to begin a line, it is followed by some object, like "Or animals," "Or birds," "Or wonderfulness." And if you look at the three lines that begin with "Every," you'll notice that each is followed by some sort of measure, as in "Every cubic inch." Taken together, these repetitions give the poem its driving rhythm. They also stitch the poem together.

WORD CHOICE

HAND OUT REPRODUCIBLE 12 "Miracles" exemplifies the work of "poet as observer." Have your students read the poem again and fill out Reproducible 12 on page 106, which asks them to consider and record details on the things that Whitman considers "miracles." Have students share some of the details they notice.

Whitman's observations are keenly described through his details, but those details would not be as effective if he had not chosen his words so carefully. Do your students notice the strong verbs he uses, particularly those that are preceded by "Or"? The expressions are fresh, not overworked. Whitman can "dart my sight over the roofs of the houses toward the sky." He can notice "the exquisite delicate thin curve of the new moon in spring." He can "wade with naked feet along the beach just in the edge of the water."

STRUCTURE

As I mentioned earlier, this poem is a list poem, which gives the poet many options when he is structuring the poem. Whitman begins and ends "Miracles" with rhetorical questions. He opens by asking, "Why, who makes much of a miracle?" and ends with "What stranger miracles are there?" In between these questions, he tries to address the opening question (not answer it) with his observation that the commonplace—like "honey-bees" and conversation with someone he loves—are miracles.

Ask your students if they remember other poems in this book or in their text that follow the same sort of bookends structure. It's a common rhetorical structure because it helps give the poem a sense of completeness and closure that is often important to the reader.

RELATED POEMS

"The Summer Day," Mary Oliver
"Birds' Nests," Ralph Fletcher
"The Blue Between," Kristine O'Connell George

Focus on the Poet

Walt Whitman (1819–1892), "the Good Gray Poet," wrote poems that praised the glories of the everyday world around him. His long, sprawling free verse poems were clearly ahead of his time when *Leaves of Grass,* his masterpiece, was published in 1855. Whitman was greatly affected by the Civil War, from the assassination of President Lincoln to the horrors he experienced as a nurse for wounded soldiers.

There are many editions of Whitman's poems. One of the most accessible is *Voyages: Poems by Walt Whitman,* selected by Lee Bennett Hopkins (Harcourt, 1988). *Leaves of Grass: A Selection of Poems and Prose* (Doubleday, 1997) is an edition of the so-called "death-bed edition" of his poems, gathered by the poet shortly before his death. Galway Kinnell stirred up controversy when he edited *The Essential Whitman* (The Ecco Press, 1987) and took the best parts from the available editions of many of the poems to create what he considered to be the best versions of Whitman's poems.

Name: _____   Date: _____

"Miracles"
Walt Whitman

AS YOU READ

1. Notice the things that Whitman considers to be "miracles." Do you think that they are miracles?

2. **Words to Know.** Here are two words that are important in the poem.

exquisite: beautifully made or designed

new moon: the phase of the moon when it is invisible or only visible as a slight crescent at sunset

AFTER YOU READ

Answer these questions:

1. What did you notice about "Miracles"? Mark up the poem with underlines, circles, and arrows to show what you noticed.

2. Do you have any questions about the poem? Jot them down.

_____

_____

_____

Poetic Terms

Here are some terms that will help you enjoy this poem:

list poem/catalog poem: a poem that is based on a list or catalog of some sort created by the poet

rhythm: the basic beat in a line of poetry

Name: _____   Date: _____

"Miracles"
Walt Whitman

In his poem, Whitman writes of the many "miracles" that surround him. Using the chart below, write down some of the things that the poet considers "miracles" and the details of the thing that make it a miracle.

MIRACLE	SPECIFIC DETAILS
example: moon	delicate, thin curve of new moon in spring

Three Short Poems

"The Apple"
Bruce Guernsey

Quartered,
a seed rocks
in each tiny cradle.

Like blood,
in the air an apple
rusts.

"Apple"
Nan Fry

At the center, a dark star
wrapped in white.
When you bite, listen
for the crunch of boots on snow,
snow that has ripened. Over it
stretches the red, starry sky.

"The Apple"
José Gorostiza
(translated by Joan Darby Norris
and Judith Infante)

Yes, the apple tastes of light,
cold light.
That's it, the apple!
What a lively fruit
so much like morning!

"The Apple," Bruce Guernsey
"Apple," Nan Fry
"The Apple," José Gorostiza

Sometimes I find short poems that I want to share with a class, but, because of their length, I worry that they may not support a sustained exploration. Then I remind myself that we need to resist believing that every time we discuss a poem, it must fill a certain amount of language arts time. There's nothing wrong with exploring a poem for a few minutes. However, for a longer exploration, short poems with similar characteristics can often be combined.

Short poems also help students realize that a poem need not be long to be effective. "Apple," for example, contains 31 words. "The Apple" by Bruce Guernsey contains only 16 words. It is quite a gift to be able to capture a scene or a feeling in so few words.

OPENERS   Before reading the poems, ask students:

1. Can you think of an object that you had looked at in one way and then suddenly saw in a new way? Perhaps there was something in your room that seemed to change when the sunlight hit it.
2. Think of a food you enjoy. Can you describe that food without referring to the sense of taste? For example, you might describe a candy cane by the sound it makes when a piece is broken off.

- Distribute the poems and have students read them silently and then in pairs or small groups. Pick at least two volunteers to read the poems to the entire class.
- Distribute the Response Sheet 13 on page 111. Ask students to answer the questions and review the poetic terms.
- Explore the poems with your class by focusing on:

THE POEMS AS A GROUP

Studying a group of similar poems shows young readers how different poets can see the same thing—like an apple—in different ways. This notion may comfort students who feel that they can't write about a particular subject because someone else has "already done that."

In addition, looking at a group of poems in which different poets handled the same subject can help young readers begin to make comparative judgments. Such discussions can be especially fruitful when students have copies of the poems in front of them and are encouraged to discuss the relative merits of the poems. After reading the poems and discussing them in class, students may be better able to judge their merits. They may, for example, feel one poem is better than another because it contains a stronger image.

DETAILS

All poets look closely—at objects, actions, emotions—and frequently notice what the average person does not. But, as readers, we can read the poems and see what the poets have noticed, which, in turn, may help us notice more carefully. Just as different poets are apt to write different types of poems about the same subject, so, too, they are likely to notice things through different senses.

HAND OUT REPRODUCIBLE 13 Give your students Reproducible 13 on page 112, which asks them to think about the senses on which these three poets rely. Guernsey notices through the sense of sight, including details about the color of the apple meat. Fry notices through her sense of sight—"a dark star/wrapped in white"—but she also notices through her sense of sound. She says, in fact, "listen/for the crunch of boots on snow." Gorostiza notices through his sense of taste, remarking of "the apple tastes of light,/cold light." Then he compares the "lively fruit" to morning: "so much like morning!"

IMAGES

Remind your students that a poet often uses comparisons, especially metaphors and similes, to create an image for the reader. This image will often be built on various senses, not just sight. While talking about these poems, your students can refer to their notes from the Reproducible.

In "The Apple," Bruce Guernsey uses only 16 words, 20 syllables. The poem is barely longer than a haiku. But look at what he has done. Each stanza holds its own image. In the first stanza, he uses the metaphor of a "tiny cradle" to show us the quartered apple rocking. Your students may notice how Guernsey uses a simile in the second stanza when he compares the color of the discolored apple meat to blood. He also uses the word "rusts" to show a color, but also to connote how the apple is slowly decomposing, much the way iron does when it oxidizes and rusts.

Fry uses several senses in "Apple." For example, she sees the "dark star/wrapped in white." And to conclude the poem, she uses a metaphor as she notices "the red, starry sky." In between these sight images, she relies on the sense of taste—"When you bite"—and the sense of hearing—"listen/for the crunch of boots on snow." These various sense impressions create Fry's image of the apple.

José Gorostiza's poem, "The Apple," weaves two senses. In the first two lines, he says that the apple "tastes of light,/cold light." So, he connects the taste with something he can see and feel. Then, in the final two lines of the poem, he continues with that image by saying that the "lively fruit" is "so much like morning," linking the "cold light" of line 2 with morning in line 5.

FORM

These short, spare poems are similar to the Imagist poems written around the time of World War I by the likes of Ezra Pound, Carl Sandburg, William Carlos Williams, and Amy Lowell. Influenced by Japanese and Chinese poetry, the Imagists revolted against the conventions of much contemporary poetry by using the language of common speech, suggesting rather than giving definitive statements, and concentrating on presenting images in the most economical way. *The Imagist Poem: Modern Poetry in Miniature,* edited by William Pratt (Story Line Press, 2001), is a classic anthology of Imagist poems. You can also look for Imagist-like poems in the individual works of the poet mentioned above.

RELATED POEMS

A trio of poems:

"Being a Kite," Jacqueline Sweeney

"I'm Up Here," Karla Kuskin

"The Kite that Braved Old Orchard Beach," X.J. Kennedy

Another trio of poems:

"Cumulus Clouds," Sheryl L. Nelms

"The Loaves," Ronald Everson

"Rags," Judith Thurman

Focus on the Poets

Bruce Guernsey teaches English at the University of Eastern Illinois. In addition to his poems that have appeared in numerous journals, he has published several books of poetry, including *January Thaw* (University of Pittsburgh Press, 1982) and *The Invention of the Telephone* (Stormline Press, 1987).

Nan Fry is a faculty member at the Corcoran School of Art in Washington, D.C. Her latest book of poems is *Relearning the Dark* (Washington Writers' Publishing House, 1991).

José Gorostiza (1901–1973) spent years working for the Mexican government in several capacities, including as secretary of foreign affairs.

Name: _____   Date: _____

Apple Poems

1. What did you notice about these three apple poems? Mark up the poems with underlines, circles, and arrows to show what you noticed.

2. Do you have any questions about these poems? Jot them down.

_____

_____

_____

_____

3. What sensory details did the poets use in these poems?

_____

_____

_____

_____

Poetic Terms

Here are some terms that will help you enjoy this poem:

stanza: a group of lines of poetry, usually similar in length and pattern

metaphor: a comparison of two dissimilar things that implies some sort of equality between the things

simile: a comparison using "like" or "as"

image: a picture the poet creates with vivid words that appeal to the reader's senses

Name: _____   Date: _____

Apple Poems

In the chart below, record some of the sensory details you noticed in these poems. In the first column, write the detail. In the second, write the sense to which it relates.

DETAIL	SENSE
example: when you bite, listen for the crunch of boots on snow	hearing

"Remember"
Christina Rossetti

Remember me when I am gone away,

Gone far away into the silent land;

When you can no more hold me by the hand,

Nor I half turn to go yet turning stay.

Remember me when no more day by day

You tell me of our future that you plann'd:

Only remember me; you understand

It will be late to counsel then or pray.

Yet if you should forget me for a while

And afterwards remember, do not grieve:

For if the darkness and corruptions leave

A vestige of the thoughts that once I had,

Better by far you should forget and smile

Than that you should remember and be sad.

EXPLORATION 14

"Remember"
Christina Rossetti

The sonnet is a form that poets have long used to write of love and love lost. In this poem, Christina Rossetti, the younger sister of Dante Gabriel Rossetti, writes of a time when she will see her lover no more. She is able to harness strong emotions and write about them convincingly within the rigid framework of a sonnet.

OPENERS   Before reading the poem, ask students:

1. Can you think of characters in books, movies, or television shows that were separated from the people they cared for? How did their situations work out in the end?

2. Have you lost someone you cared for? How did you deal with the loss?

- Distribute Response Sheet 14 on page 117 and ask students to review the "words to know" in the "As You Read" section.

- Distribute the poem and have students read it silently and then in pairs or small groups. Pick at least two volunteers to read the poem to the entire class.

- Have students complete the "After You Read" section of Response Sheet 14.

- Explore the poem with your class by focusing on:

FORM

The sonnet originated in Italy in the thirteenth century with the work of Dante and Petrach. It was brought to England about 300 years later in the 1530s when Sir Thomas Wyatt discovered sonnets while visiting Italy and Spain. Although the sonnet form was not immediately popular in England, it did begin to gain acceptance in the Elizabethan age when Shakespeare was working on his 154 sonnets.

   The sonnet is a 14-line poem, generally written in iambic pentameter. That is, lines with five iambic feet, which is made up of an unstressed syllable followed by a stressed syllable, as in the words *until, before,* and *prefer.* So, each line in a sonnet will contain 10 syllables, with the stress falling on every other syllable. There are, of course, variations to this "rule." Here are the opening two lines from Sonnet 22 by Shakespeare:

114

My glass shall not persuade me I am old
So long as youth and you are of one date

As far as structure is concerned, there are two kinds of sonnets: Shakespearean or Elizabethan and the Italian or Petrarchan. Although both, of course, contain 14 lines, the organization of the lines and the rhyme schemes are different. The Shakespearean sonnet is written with three quatrains, or groups of four lines, and a couplet, which is reflected in the rhyme scheme: *abab cdcd efef gg*. On the other hand, the Italian sonnet is written in one octave (eight lines, often two quatrains) and a sestet (six lines), with a rhyme scheme of *abba cddc efg efg*. It is important to recognize that there are variations of this pattern. "Remember," in fact, is a modified Italian sonnet. You can see that the rhyme scheme is *abba abba cddece*.

When young students explore a structured poem, like the sonnet, I think it's reasonable that they hear the rhythm of the iambic pentameter lines. And that they recognize the rhyme scheme. However, it seems inappropriate that they be given the names of the assorted metric feet to memorize and poems to scan.

STRUCTURE

HAND OUT REPRODUCIBLE 14 Before you have your students read "Remember" aloud, ask them to be on the lookout for structural elements in the poem. Can they notice any breaks in the sense of the poem or in its narrative flow? Does the poet change her line of thinking? With careful reading, your students may see that this sonnet is broken into two quatrains and a sestet. Each quatrain begins with the same words: "Remember me when." Reproducible 14 on page 118 should help them visualize the three parts of the poem. Each quatrain tells how and when the poet wants to be remembered:

Lines 1–4: Remember me when… when I'm gone far away, when you can no longer hold my hand, nor I, ready to leave, turn and stay.

Lines 5–8: Remember me when… when you no longer talk of our future together, when it is too late to talk or pray.

Notice how the sestet begins with a transitional word, "Yet" (in other words, "on the other hand"), and the poet continues to say that if you should forget me, that's okay because it's "Better by far" that you forget me and smile than remember me and "be sad."

REPETITION

You've seen in a number of poems in this book how repetition is a way for the poet to tie the poem together. That's exactly what Rossetti does in this poem. Your students can see how she uses the word "remember" five times in the poem, including the first and the final line. Three times she uses the phrase "remember me." And, for emphasis, she uses "gone away" and "Gone far away" in the first two lines and she repeats the phrase "no more" early in the poem. These repetitions emphasize the notion of a final separation.

RELATED POEMS

Three sonnets:

"Time does not bring relief; you all have lied," Edna
    St. Vincent Millay

"Frederick Douglas," Robert Hayden

"Dreamers," Siegfried Sassoon

Focus on the Poet

Christina Rossetti (1830–1894) was the youngest of four children of an Italian scholar who moved to London six years before she was born. After she broke off two engagements because of religious differences between her and her fiancés, she settled into a life typical for unmarried middle-class women of the time. She also spent much of her time socializing with some of the important literary and artistic men of her time, like Whistler, Swinburne, and Dodgson (a.k.a. Lewis Carroll). Rossetti wrote poetry for most of her life, much of it inspired by her religion. Most critics consider *Goblin Market* (1862) to be her most important work.

You can find more information about her and other pre-Raphaelite women at <victorian web.org/crossetti/crov.html>. Her work is also included in the web site of Sonnet Central, <www.sonnets.org/rossettc.htm>.

Name: _____ Date: _____

"Remember," Christina Rossetti

AS YOU READ

Words to Know. Here are some words that are important in the poem.

counsel: advise or guide; *corruption:* dishonest, tainted; *vestige:* a visible trace, remnant

AFTER YOU READ

Answer these questions:

1. What did you notice about "Remember"? Mark up the poem with underlines, circles, and arrows to show what you noticed.

2. Do you have any questions about this poem? Jot them down.

_____

_____

3. How do you think the poet feels in this poem?

_____

_____

Poetic Terms

Here are some terms that will help you enjoy this poem:

sonnet: a 14-line poem written in iambic pentameter that follows a particular rhyme scheme

iambic pentameter: a poetic line of five iambic feet (i.e. an unaccented syllable followed by an accented syllable, as in words such as *beware, until,* and *respond*).

couplet: two lines of poetry that rhyme

quatrain: a poem (or portion of a poem) or stanza of four lines

sestet: a poem (or portion of a poem) or stanza of six lines

rhyme scheme: the pattern of end rhymes in a poem

Name: _____ Date: _____

"Remember"
Christina Rossetti

A sonnet of this sort is divided into three parts. As you read the poem, be on the lookout for those three parts and, in the boxes below, write Rossetti's main idea for each part in your own words.

"Noise"

Janet S. Wong

Ching chong Chinaman

    Those kids over there
    are laughing at me.
    My hair.
    My nose.
    My skin.

    I hear the noise.
Ching chong
    I won't let it in.

    They're pulling their lids
    up, down and out
    to the side,
    making wide eyes slit thin,
    faking being
    some kind of Chinese
    I've never seen,
    chanting

       [stanza break]

Ching chong ching chong
Open your eyes
Open your eyes, Chinese

    It's only noise.
Ching chong
    I won't let it in.
    I won't let it in.

    I promise myself

    I won't let them
    win.

EXPLORATION 15

"Noise"
Janet S. Wong

We've all had childhood experiences that have stuck with us, in one way or another. "Cottontail" tells of unpleasant experience. In "Noise," Janet S. Wong writes about the cruel taunts she endured from some of her schoolmates because she had Chinese features. Her poem is a clear expression of her anger and frustration.

OPENERS Before reading the poem, ask students:

1. Have you ever been teased by other kids? For what reason? How did it make you feel?

2. Have you ever teased another kid? (This includes your siblings!) For what reason? How did it make you feel?

• Distribute the poem and have students read it silently and then in pairs or small groups. Pick at least two volunteers to read the poem to the entire class.

• Distribute the Response Sheet 15 on page 123. Ask students to answer the questions.

• Explore the poem with your class by focusing on:

STRUCTURE

"Noise" is almost a poem in two voices, and Wong structures the poem on the page so we can see that. Note how the indented stanzas are her own thoughts, for example "Those kids over there/are laughing at me" and "I won't let them in./I won't let them in." Not only do we learn what the narrator is thinking and feeling, we also get a glimpse of what her tormentors are doing: "They're pulling their lids/up and down/…making wide eyes slit thin." The six remaining lines that begin closer to the left-hand margin are the taunts of her classmates: "Ching chong Chinaman" and the like.

HAND OUT REPRODUCIBLE 15 The structure makes the poem perfect for choral reading. Ask for one student to read the narrator's part and have a section of the class read in unison the other parts. Setting up the reading in this way will help the class see the unfairness of the situation, with one lone reader standing against the large chanting group. Before you try this, however, make sure the student who reads the narrator's part understands how the narrator felt. The student must read with appropriate emotion. Since the narrator is very angry, the oral reading of the girl's part must reflect that. To help your class come to a clearer understanding of the dynamics of the situation in the poem, have them complete Reproducible 15 on page 124, which asks them to examine what is said and done in the poem.

SOUND

A choral reading of the poem as I outlined above should give your students a better understanding of the chant nature of this poem. Ask your students if they can remember a time when they chanted as a group. Perhaps they will recall a sporting event. Or, perhaps some camping activity with Scouts. Discussing such friendly chants will set up a strong contrast when they see how Wong begins the poem with a taunting, nasty chant: "Ching chong Chinaman," a phrase that appears four other times in the poem. Wong also repeats the word *my* many times in the poem, as if she is emphasizing her individuality. Also, perhaps it shows how she felt alienated from other members of the class.

The short lines in the poem will sound choppy, but they also better convey the anger and frustration that the narrator feels. These short lines are almost spit out by the narrator. In addition, look at the spaces in the poem, especially toward the end of the poem. With a slight pause at every space between lines of the poem, we can almost feel the narrator trying to retain her composure:

> It's only noise.
> Ching chong
> I won't let it in.
> I won't let it in.
>
> I promise myself
> I won't let them
> win.

Notice how the line "I won't let it in" is used three times and the final line of the poem is a variation of that line: "I won't let them/win." This sort of repetition helps to create that chant feeling in the poem. And, when you're thinking about that final repetition, notice how the final word "win" rhymes with "in." Adding to the chant effect of the poem is the repetition of the *ch* sound at the start of the taunt, "Ching chong Chinaman."

WORD CHOICE

Sometimes the title of a poem is important to the overall effect of the poem. Such is the case with "Cottontail," and I think the title is important to this poem. By calling the poem "Noise," Wong might be saying that she didn't want to dignify what the other kids were chanting by calling it other than what it really was: *noise.* That word also appears twice in the poem.

Using simple language, Wong gives us a clear image of what the scene is like. "Those kids over there/are laughing at me," she tells us. We can hear them. They're laughing at her appearance. A bit later in the poem, she paints a visual picture of what the other children are doing: pulling on their eye lids, making "eyes slit thin." But it is the repeated taunt—"Ching chong Chinaman"—that assaults our ears and gives us a loud image of how cruel her schoolmates are.

RELATED POEMS

"Incident," Countee Cullen
"Waiting at the Railroad Cafe," Janet S. Wong
"Blubber Lips," Jim Daniels

Focus on the Poet

Janet S. Wong was born in Los Angeles to an immigrant Chinese father and an immigrant Korean mother. After receiving her law degree from Yale, she returned to the West Coast to practice corporate and labor law for a few years. Soon, however, she decided that she was better suited to writing books and poems for children. She has published a number of poetry collections for children, including: *Night Garden: Poems from the World of Dreams; The Rainbow Hand: Poems About Mothers And Children; Behind the Wheel: Poems about Driving* (all from Simon & Schuster).

To find out more about Janet Wong and listen to her read from her work, you can go to her web site: <janetwong.com>.

Name: _____ Date: _____

"Noise"
Janet S. Wong

1. What did you notice about "Noise"? Mark up the poem with underlines, circles, and arrows to show what you noticed.

2. Do you have any questions about this poem? Jot them down.

_____

_____

_____

_____

3. How do the children in class treat the narrator of the poem? How does the narrator react? Don't forget to be specific.

_____

_____

_____

_____

Poetic Terms

Here are two terms that will help you enjoy this poem:

refrain: a word or phrase that is repeated throughout the poem

alliteration: repetition of vowel sounds, usually at the beginning of words

Name: _____ Date: _____

"Noise"
Janet S. Wong

After carefully listening to the poem, note in the spaces below some important things:

1. How do the children treat the narrator?

2. What do they say and do?

3. How does it make the narrator feel?

4. How does she react to her classmates?

PART 3:
Becoming an Active Reader of Poetry: Advice and Resources

How can you become a reader of poetry? The answer is quite simple: read poetry. While it's important to read lots of poems so we can find the best examples to share with our students, it's also important to read lots of poems on our own. We need to read poems that we would never think of bringing to a class, perhaps because the subject matter is too adult. Or the language might be offensive to or too advanced for some members of the community. Only when we are moved by poetry can we share those feelings with our students. Only when we are moved, as Emily Dickinson was when she said that she knows she's read poetry when "it makes my whole body so cold no fire can ever warm me, [when] I feel physically as if the top of my head were taken off," can we hope for that sensation for our students. "These are the only ways I know it," she wrote. "Is there any other way?"

In a country that boasts 2.2 million accordion players, it seems that poetry should have more readers than it does. Why don't more people read poetry? I think they are afraid of it. Afraid they won't be able to "figure it out," as if it were one of those infernal word problems about two trains traveling in opposite directions at different rates of speed. As if poetry had a "message" that the reader needed to find. As if experiencing a poem was somehow not enough, somehow intellectually inferior to cutting into it to find its "message." United States Poet Laureate Billy Collins captures the essence of this problem in his poem "Introduction to Poetry":

> I ask them to take a poem
> and hold it up to the light
> like a color slide
>
> or press an ear against its hive.
> [stanza break]

I say drop a mouse into a poem
and watch him probe his way out,

or walk inside the poem's room
and feel the walls for a light switch.

I want them to waterski
across the surface of a poem
waving at the author's name on the shore.

But all they want to do
is tie the poem to a chair with rope
and torture a confession out of it.

They begin beating it with a hose
to find out what it really means.

Here are some suggestions for making poetry a central part of your life and weaving it into teaching on an ongoing basis:

Start Where You Are

When you are ready to read more poetry, start in your comfort zone. That might mean reading some favorite poems you recall from college or childhood—poems your parents might have read to you, or, if the "classic" poems are not your taste, go for contemporary poets. Start with an anthology. Pick any anthology. Pick it for its title or the eye-catching cover art. Or because it's edited by someone you admire. After editing more than 20 anthologies myself, I've come to see an anthology as a buffet where you see all kinds of offerings arrayed before your eyes. Some are common and safe. Others are new and exotic. After considering the options, you decide: a little of this, a little of that, maybe a lot of this other thing. When you find something you like, you come back for more. It's the same thing with a poetry anthology: You sample the work of many poets—a little Mary Oliver, a smattering of Seamus Heaney, a bit of Maya Angelou—find what appeals to you, then go back for more. Lots more.

Read for Yourself...and for Your Students

Even if you are intentionally looking for children's poems, read for yourself. Read for the poems that will satisfy you. Don't hesitate to teach appropriate poems by "adult" poets. As an anthologist, it gives me great pride to introduce children to poets who have never written specifically for the "children's market." *Seeing the Blue Between: Advice and Inspiration for Young Writers,* my latest anthology, contains work by Mark Vinz, Liz Rosenberg, Andrew Hudgins, Robert Farnsworth, and Christine Hemp. All of them are published poets who have not published a book of poems for children. Introducing kids to the work of adult poets is one way to nurture and enhance their tastes.

As you read more poetry in a book by, say, Mary Oliver, Paul Zimmer, or William Matthews, you will find buried treasures. You'll find poems that you enjoy and, perhaps, want to share with colleagues and friends. Your sense of poetry will deepen, allowing you to read poetry with an open mind, more open than when you were "supposed" to like a poem because a teacher told you it was written by an award-winning poet.

As you find poems suitable for your students, poems that will enrich their time in your class, you will broaden your own knowledge of poetry. And that doesn't mean only poems that are part of a longer unit of study. It also means poems that you cared for enough to read them aloud to students, perhaps as a way to begin class or to send students on their way before a holiday.

The more poems you read, the more you'll come to understand form. For example, after reading "The Red Gloves" on page 57, you'll be more likely to recognize other persona poems in your reading, such as "Broom" by Tony Johnston or "Old Elm Speaks" by Kristine O'Connell George. Save suitable poems according to form—persona poems, poems of address, list poems, odes, to name a few—and you will soon have hefty folders of examples to share with your students. As you read more poetry, you will find yourself on the lookout for poems you can adopt and welcome into your files.

Keep Current...or Befriend a Librarian

We all know that middle school teachers have much more work than they should have. It's impossible to stay current in every subject that touches your students. You need all the help you can get. Staying current in poetry for young readers is no exception. If you are nuts about poetry, the task is a bit easier because, most likely, you already read new poetry for yourself. However, if you are not, let me offer this advice: Ask a librarian.

Most school librarians know trade books better than most classroom teachers. That's the way it should be. It's part of their job, after all. They know which books are hot, which books work with kids. Librarians know which books have been recognized with awards and prizes. I'm fortunate to have as friends a number of top-notch, poetry-loving librarians who are always feeding me book tips, especially on new poetry titles. They're always willing to answer my questions. For example, after I noticed some books advertised as "novels in verse," I e-mailed librarian friends, asking for some titles that I ought to read in this genre. They all responded with recommendations. Librarians are like that: always willing to help. Good librarians do more than check out books, rearrange tables and chairs, and transport VCRs from room to room. They are invaluable when it comes to choosing books and authors. So, find a good librarian, make a friend, and talk about poetry books.

Become an Anthologist

Without knowing it, I began my career as a poetry anthologist in my first year of teaching, when I started copying poems and sticking them into files. I created several expanding files, bulging with poems. As I worked more and more with poetry in the classroom, I started organizing those poems into theme/topic files. Eventually, through the good fortune of meeting M. Jerry Weiss, who was the founder of the Laurel Leaf imprint at Dell, those bulging files became my first anthology, *The Crystal Image*.

What's to stop you from making a collection of your favorite poems? Don't limit your selections to poems that you can use with your students. Collecting good poems for your classroom is important, of course, but learning to love poetry is really about you as much as it is about the kids. When you lose your heart in a Mary Oliver poem or smile knowingly at an Andrew Hudgins poem, that experience will inform your teaching. So, keep your eyes and heart open for poems that touch you.

A good poem can touch me in many ways. Maybe the poem will get a snicker, a belly laugh. J. Patrick Lewis, X.J. Kennedy, and Jack Prelutsky can do that. So can Douglas Florian. Maybe the poem will touch me like a hand on my shoulder in troubled times. Naomi Shihab Nye and Pablo Neruda touch me that way. So do Karen Hesse and Ashley Bryan. Perhaps a poem's good ending will surprise me. David McCord is a master surpriser. But at the core of every good poem, every poem that touches me, is the language. More often than not, it's simple, ordinary language that a good poet will use in inventive ways that frequently hold meanings beyond the words themselves: language that surprises the reader, language that lets a good poem sing.

So get a three-ring binder and start using it as a poetry bank for making regular deposits. Only allow the very best poems into your collection. Don't worry about organizing them at this stage. Just read and save. When you have enough poems, start adding section dividers. Label each section, but be open to change. Your anthology is always a work in progress. You can add, rearrange, and toss poems that no longer touch you.

As your collection grows, you might find yourself adding sticky notes to some poems, maybe to cross reference them according to form—marking this one a sonnet or that one a poem of address, for example. You might make reference to other poems with a similar subject, like the three apple poems I used in Explorations. Or, how "Lullaby" by Steve Kowit can be used with "Song for Susannah: A Lullaby" by Doris Hardie. Don't forget to refer students to other poems which may not be in your anthology but in another source, such as their textbook.

A benchmark that tells me I've found a great poem is when I get the immediate desire to share it: fax a copy to my wife at work, stick it at the end of my e-mails as a "signature," or read it aloud to my daughter before she goes to sleep. Great poems must be shared. And, if you're lucky, as I've been, you'll find people who will share their favorite poems with you. Even your students. As you read and share more poems with your kids and allow them to explore poetry, they may gain the confidence to share their own favorites with the class.

Scour All Sources

There are three primary places to look for poems: books, the Internet, audio programs. I'm a "book person," so I will always look first to them. My office walls are lined with books, mostly poetry titles that I've collected over the years. For my money, clicking your mouse and scrolling through poems doesn't evoke the same intense feeling you get from taking a book from a shelf (or a stack on the floor) and slowly turning its pages. True, the Internet does offer lightning quick searches and nearly limitless choices. But, somehow, when I'm looking for a poem, I prefer the old-fashioned method. So, let me start by suggesting some books that will offer you rich poetic experiences.

Poetry Books

As I mentioned in Part 2, a sensible place to start reading poetry is an anthology. A good anthology breaks ground. It offers many poets that you can explore more fully. Pick any of the anthologies on the following list and feel confident that you'll find some poems that will excite you.

The list is meant to be a starting point for you and your students, or for anyone who might be timid about reading poetry. I selected these books the same way I select poems for my anthologies, by including the books with poems that speak to me. You are not going to like every poem in every book. And, surely, neither will your students. The point is not to like every poem, but to read every poem with, to use a Zen phrase, "a beginner's mind." I've divided the list into four categories:

• anthologies that seem appropriate for younger students, grades 4–6
• anthologies better suited for older students, grades 7 and up
• books by individual poets appropriate for younger students, grades 4–6
• books by individual poets appropriate for older students, grades 7 and up

However, since you know your students better than anyone else, don't limit yourself to one list. For example, if you teach grades 4 to 6, begin with the first list, but don't ignore the books on the 7-and-up list. You will most likely find poems in young adult books that will work well with your younger readers. Likewise, some of your older students might enjoy poems written for "children."

ANTHOLOGIES

FOR YOUNGER STUDENTS, GRADES 4–6

A Caribbean Dozen: Poems from Caribbean Poets edited by John Agard and Grace Nichols, Candlewick, 1994. A vibrant collection of word and color, this book's pages dance before your eyes.

Dreams of Glory: Poems Starring Girls edited by Isabel Joshlin Glaser, Atheneum, 1995. The perfect collection of poems that show what girls can do.

The Rattle Bag edited by Seamus Heaney and Ted Hughes, Faber & Faber, 1982. This comprehensive collection of mostly British and American poems offers something for all readers.

Hand in Hand: An American History through Poetry edited by Lee Bennett Hopkins, Simon and Schuster, 1994. This collection will speak to kids in language arts class or social studies class. It goes nicely with *We, the People,* by Bobbi Katz. (See below.)

Opening Day: Sports Poems edited by Lee Bennett Hopkins, Harcourt, 1996. A good collection of accessible poems that may prove irresistible to some reluctant boy readers.

Dirty Laundry Pile: Poems in Different Voices edited by Paul B. Janeczko, HarperCollins, 2001. The subjects of the persona, or mask, poems in this collection speak in different voices.

The Place My Words Are Looking For edited by Paul B. Janeczko, Simon and Schuster, 1990. Some of the most popular children's poets speak about their craft in this collection of poems and short essays written specifically for this book.

Poetry from A to Z: A Guide for Young Writers edited by Paul B. Janeczko, Simon and Schuster, 1994. In addition to being an anthology of accessible poems, it is also something of an instructional book with a dozen poetry writing instruction and activities.

A Poke in the Eye: A Collection of Concrete Poems edited by Paul B. Janeczko, Candlewick, 2001. Chris Raschka's amazing illustrations make these concrete poems come alive.

Seeing the Blue Between: Advice and Inspiration for Young Writers edited by Paul B. Janeczko, Candlewick, 2002. An anthology of poems augmented by letters written by the poets to the young readers of the book.

Stone Bench in an Empty Park edited by Paul B. Janeczko, Orchard, 2000. This collection of haiku with an urban setting is illustrated with stunning photos.

Very Best (Almost) Friends edited by Paul B. Janeczko, Candlewick, 1999. The poems in this anthology examine friendship from different perspectives.

Knock at a Star: A Child's Introduction to Poetry edited by X. J. Kennedy and Dorothy M. Kennedy, Little, Brown, 1999. Like *Poetry from A to Z,* this book is part anthology, part writing book.

Animal, Vegetable, Mineral: Poems About Small Things edited by Myra Cohn Livingston, HarperCollins, 1994. Livingston reminds young readers that poetry is about paying attention.

The Tree Is Older Than You Are: A Bilingual Gathering of Poems and Stories from Mexico with Paintings by Mexican Artists edited by Naomi Shihab Nye, Simon and Schuster, 1995. The mile-long subtitle notwithstanding, this is a stunning collection of word and color.

This Same Sky: A Collection of Poems from Around the World edited by Naomi Shihab Nye, Simon and Schuster, 1995. Nye's first anthology, this collection is still a joyful magic carpet ride around the world.

Celebrate America in Poetry and Art edited by Nora Panzer, Hyperion, 1994. A rich collection that matches poems with works of art and celebrates the cultural and artistic diversity of our country.

Singing America: Poems That Define a Nation edited by Neil Philip, Viking, 1995. A good selection of poems, crisply illustrated with black-and-white wood cuts.

For Laughing Out Loud: Poems to Tickle Your Funnybone edited by Jack Prelutsky, Knopf, 1991. The subtitle says it all.

The Random House Book of Poetry for Children edited by Jack Prelutsky, Random House, 1983. A classic, this comprehensive collection for all ages is enhanced with the illustrations of Arnold Lobel.

For Older Students, Grades 7 and Up

I Am the Darker Brother: An Anthology of Modern Poems by African Americans edited by Arnold Adoff, Simon and Schuster, 1997. Adoff's collection of modern poems deserves to have a place in your shelf.

The Poetry of Black America: Anthology of the 20th Century edited by Arnold Adoff, HarperCollins, 1973. A comprehensive collection, from DuBois and Dunbar to Giovanni and Troupe and beyond.

Mountain Rivers: Vietnamese Poetry from the Wars, 1948-1973, edited by Kevin Bowen, Nguyen Ba Chung, and Bruce Weigl, University of Massachusetts Press, 1998. A substantial bilingual collection of 79 poems, biographical information, and a selected reading list.

Songs from this Earth on Turtle's Back edited by Joseph Bruchac, Greenfield Review Press, 1983. Including the work of 52 poets from more than 35 Native American nations, Bruchac gives a glimpse of the many voices of Native Americans.

Poetry After Lunch: Poems to Read Aloud edited by Joyce Armstrong Carroll and Edward E. Wilson, Absey & Co., 1997. Celebrating the act of reading poetry aloud, these contemporary poems will strike a responsive chord with kids.

Cool Salsa: Bilingual Poems on Growing Up Latino in the United States edited by Lori M. Carlson, Holt, 1994. There are many new voices in this book that deserve to be heard.

I Wouldn't Thank You for a Valentine: Poems for Young Feminists edited by Carol Ann Duffy, Holt, 1994. A slim volume packed with the energetic voices of women from different cultures.

Reflections of a Gift of Watermelon Pickle...and Other Modern Verse edited by Stephen Dunning, Edward Lueders, et. al., Scott Foresman, 1995. A revised edition of the classic that started it all for me and still a wonderful book of poems and photographs.

Shimmy Shimmy Shimmy Like My Sister Kate: Looking at the Harlem Renaissance Through Poetry edited by Nikki Giovanni, Holt, 1996. More than a collection of Harlem Renaissance poetry, this book includes the work of more recent African American poets, like Sonia Sanchez and Ntozake Shange.

After Aztlan: Latino Poets of the Nineties edited by Ray Gonzalez, Godine, 1992. From Francisco Alarcon to Tino Villanueva, this is the first comprehensive poetry anthology of Latino poets who write primarily in English.

The School Bag edited by Seamus Heaney and Ted Hughes, Faber & Faber, 1997. A companion to *The Rattle Bag,* this collection is arranged thematically and features poets who write in English, including poets of Scotland, Ireland, and Wales.

Preposterous: Poems of Youth edited by Paul B. Janeczko, Orchard, 1991. A collection that features the voices from those tough adolescent years.

Looking for Your Name: A Collection of Contemporary Poems edited by Paul B. Janeczko, Orchard, 1993. This collection makes a statement about life in contemporary America and life in the heart. My most "political" anthology.

Wherever Home Begins: 100 Contemporary Poems edited by Paul B. Janeczko, Orchard, 1995. A collection of poems about place and its significance to us as human creatures.

Best-Loved Poems of Jacqueline Kennedy Onassis edited by Caroline Kennedy, Random House, 2001. A well-balanced and broad panorama of poems for young and old.

American Sports Poems edited by R.R. Knudson and May Swenson, Orchard, 1988. This is still a strong collection that includes the work of many fine poets, from Whitman and Sandburg to Updike and Silverstein.

I Feel a Little Jumpy Aroud You: A Book of Her Poems and His Poems Collected in Pairs edited by Naomi Shihab Nye and Paul B. Janeczko, Simon and Schuster, 1996. A unique collection that sheds light on the way men and women see the world.

The Space Between Our Footsteps: Poems and Paintings from the Middle East edited by Naomi Shihab Nye, Simon and Schuster, 1998. Like *The Tree Is Older Than You Are* (see above) this book is a masterpiece in words and pictures.

What Have You Lost? edited by Naomi Shihab Nye, Greenwillow, 1999. Over 100 poems that explore the things we lose and find.

Earth-Shattering Poems edited by Liz Rosenberg, Holt, 1997. As in *Light-Gathering Poems,* Rosenberg has selected intense poems, but here are many that don't often find their way into anthologies.

Light-Gathering Poems edited by Liz Rosenberg, Holt, 2000. Poems of passion and yearning, of birth and death. All are poems of hurt and healing.

Imaginary Gardens: American Poetry and Art for Young People edited by Charles Sullivan, Abrams, 1989. Like *Celebrate America in Poetry and Art* (see above), this collection nicely matches America's art with its poetry.

Truth & Lies edited by Patrice Vecchione, Holt, 2001. Gathering poems from different eras and cultures, this collection explores the relationship between being truthful and telling lies.

BOOKS BY INDIVIDUAL POETS

Reading a book of poetry by an individual poet should be an act of discovery about that poet and his or her work. These lists are by no means exhaustive or comprehensive, but they will give you and your students an introduction to the work of many fine poets. My hope is, of course, that you will hustle over to your library and check out other books by these poets.

FOR YOUNGER STUDENTS, GRADES 4–6

Everywhere Faces Everywhere by James Berry, Simon and Schuster, 1997.

The Earth Under Sky Bear's Feet: Native American Poems of the Land by Joseph Bruchac, Philomel, 1995.

Sing to the Sun by Ashley Bryan, Harper, 1992.

Rich Lizard and Other Poems by Deborah Chandra, Farrar, 1993.

Peacock Pie by Walter de la Mare, Holt, 1989.

Who Shrank My Grandmother's House: Poems of Discovery by Barbara Juster Esbensen, Harper, 1992.

Joyful Noise: Poems for Two Voices by Paul Fleischman, Harper, 1988.

Ordinary Things: Poems from a Walk in Early Spring by Ralph Fletcher, Atheneum, 1997.

Laugh-eteria by Douglas Florian, Harcourt, 1999.

Fly with Poetry: An ABC of Poetry by Avis Harley, Wordsong, 2000.

Out of the Dust by Karen Hesse, Scholastic, 1997.

Witness by Karen Hess, Scholastic, 2001.

The Dream Keeper and Other Poems by Langston Hughes, Knopf, 1994.

That Sweet Diamond: Baseball Poems by Paul B. Janeczko, Atheneum, 1998.

The Other Side: Shorter Poems by Angela Johnson, Orchard, 1998.

We, The People by Bobbi Katz, Harper, 2000.

Exploding Gravy: Poems to Make You Laugh by X.J. Kennedy, Little, Brown, 2002.

A Tree Place and Other Poems by Constance Levy, McElderry, 1994.

Riddle-lightful by J. Patrick Lewis, Knopf, 1998.

One at a Time by David McCord, Little, Brown, 1977.

Ogden Nash's Zoo by Ogden Nash, Stewart, Tabori & Chang, 1987.

Come With Me: Poems for a Journey by Naomi Shihab Nye, Greenwillow, 2000.

Awful Ogre's Awful Day by Jack Prelutsky, Greenwillow, 2001.

Waiting to Waltz by Cynthia Rylant, Bradbury, 1984.

Advice for a Frog by Alice Schertle, Lothrop, 1995.

A Lucky Thing by Alice Schertle, Browndeer, 1999.

Laughing Time: Collected Nonsense by William Jay Smith, Farrar, 1990.

Canto Familiar by Gary Soto, Harcourt, 1995.

Neighborhood Odes by Gary Soto, Harcourt, 1992.

Popcorn by James Stevenson, Greenwillow, 1998

The Pig in the Spigot by Richard Wilbur, Harcourt 2000.

A Suitcase of Seaweed and Other Poems by Janet S. Wong, McElderry, 1996.

All the Small Poems and Fourteen More by Valerie Worth, Farrar, 1994.

- -

FOR OLDER STUDENTS, GRADES 7 AND UP

Selected Poems by Gwendolyn Brooks, Harper, 1990.

Frenchtown Summer by Robert Cormier, Delacorte, 1999.

I Am Wings: Poems About Love by Ralph Fletcher, Atheneum, 1994.

My Friend's Got This Problem, Mr. Chandler: High School Poems by Mel Glenn, Clarion, 1991.

Stepping Out With Grandma Mac by Nikki Grimes, Orchard, 2001.

Polaroid and Other Poems by Betsy Hearne, Harper, 1995.

Collected Poems by Langston Hughes, Random House, 1994.

Running Back to Ludie by Angela Johnson, Scholastic, 2001.

The Brimstone Journals by Ron Koertge, Candlewick, 2001.

The Inner City Mother Goose by Eve Merriam, Simon and Schuster, 1996.

Carver: A Life in Poems by Marilyn Nelson, Front Street, 2001.

Scuppernong by Brenda Seabrooke, Cobblehill, 1990.

Girl Coming in for a Landing by April Wayland, Knopf, 2002.

Behind the Wheel: Poems About Driving by Janet S. Wong, Simon and Schuster, 1999.

Here are the names of poets who do not specifically write for young adults, but whose work contains poems that will speak to adolescents. I encourage you to explore these poets and see what they have to offer your students and you.

Jimmy Santiago Baca	Joy Harjo	Stanley Kunitz	William Stafford
Lucille Clifton	Jane Hirschfield	Robert Morgan	John Updike
Jim Daniels	David Huddle	Pablo Neruda	Mark Vinz
Cornelius Eady	June Jordan	Naomi Shihab Nye	Paul Zimmer
Robert Francis	Jane Kenyon	Mary Oliver	
Gary Gildner	Ron Koertge	Linda Pastan	
Donald Hall	Maxine Kumin	Liz Rosenberg	

Web Sites

The Internet has certainly increased the amount of information available to us. But, "more" is not necessarily "good," especially when the information is not subject to any sort of scrutiny. Your students need to understand that anyone can build a web page and load it with misleading or plain incorrect information—information about anything from abortion to sonnets. Anyone can also build a web site and fill it with dreadful poetry. Nonetheless, there are many web sites that have been thoughtfully constructed. The web sites that I have included on this list are reputable sites. They offer you and your students plenty of good poems, as well as solid information about poetry and poets.

POETRY 180 (www.loc.gov/poetry/180)

This site is a project originated by Billy Collins, Poet Laureate of the United States. The 180 in the title reflects the intent of the site: "a poem a day for American high schools." But as Collins says, the "180-degree turn implies a turning back—in this case, to poetry." He says that the idea behind this site is simple: "to have a poem read each day to the students in American high schools across the country." Equally simple is the goal of the program: "to give students a chance to listen to a poem each day." Note how Collins rightfully puts an emphasis on reading aloud and listening to poetry. He even includes a link to some suggestions on how to read a poem aloud.

In addition to including the 180 poems he suggests be read to the kids, the site also answers some of the questions teachers might have about it, such as "How should the poems be presented?" and "When do we start?" Collins hopes that listening to contemporary poems "might convince students that poetry can be an understandable, painless and even eye-opening part of their everyday experience." Hooray for Billy Collins. And hooray for those teachers who are willing to try the program.

One of the admirable things about this site is that the poems in the program—all on the site and all printable—are written by well-known poets—like Jane Kenyon, Lucille Clifton, Robert Bly, and Donald Justice—as well as by lesser-known poets, like Kay Ryan, Eve Shockley, Mac Hammond, and Shara McCallum. What a exciting way to meet new poets. Although the site is for high-school students, I wouldn't let that stop you from checking it out for poems that would be appropriate to use with younger kids. I would certainly consider using "Daybreak" by Galway Kinnell or "The Summer I Was Sixteen" by Geraldine Connolly with most middle-school kids. And, if you can't find poems that you think will work with the kids in your school, why not suggest to your colleagues that they each find a dozen poems that are suitable and begin your own original Poetry 180.

FAVORITE POEM PROJECT (www.favoritepoem.org)

This site has a couple of things in common with Poetry 180. For one thing, it was originated by a Poet Laureate of the United States, Robert Pinsky. Secondly, the emphasis at this site is on reading poetry and listening to poetry read aloud. According to Pinksy, reading a poem silently instead of reading it aloud is like "the difference between staring at a sheet of music and actually humming or playing the music on an instrument."

When Pinksy was named the 39th Poet Laureate in 1997, he created the Favorite Poem Project. His idea started small. He and a friend wandered around Washington D.C. with a "fancy tape recorder," asking people to read a poem aloud. The idea took off and evolved into a project that encouraged live readings in communities across the country. To date, the project has produced a set of 50 short videos of individuals reading their favorite poems; an anthology, *America's Favorite Poems* (Norton, 2000); and a searchable database of 18,000 letters detailing favorite poems and personal responses to them. There is also, of course, the web site, which features audio and video clips of people reading their favorite poems. Like the poems included in Poetry 180, the poems at this site are printable. However, unlike Poetry 180, the poems read in the Favorite Poem Project include poems by "classic" authors, including the likes of Chaucer, Dickinson, Housman, and Longfellow.

Another thing that the Favorite Poem Project has in common with Poetry 180 is that it could easily serve as a model for a similar project in your school and in your community. Find out who has a favorite poem. Ask the students, of course, but don't stop there. Explore other possibilities. The principal, the bus driver, the person who runs the corner laundromat, the cop on the beat. Do they have a favorite poem? Would they be willing to read it aloud into a tape recorder? Start with some people you suspect would happily read their favorite poem into the tape recorder. Like Pinsky's program, yours will grow in time, producing a valuable archive of spoken poetry.

FOOLING WITH WORDS WITH BILL MOYER (www.pbs.org/wnet/foolingwithwords)
Based on the 1998 PBS special, "Fooling with Words with Bill Moyers," this site celebrates the spoken word at the 1998 Geraldine R. Dodge Poetry Festival. Like the festival itself, this site recognizes the importance of giving spoken poetry an audience. As poet Mark Doty put it, "The act of making a poem requires that somebody's listening." Among the two dozen poets you can view and listen to at this site are Galway Kinnell, Robert Pinsky, Lorna Dee Cervantes, and Lucille Clifton.

Although the poems are more appropriate for older students, the site does offer a lot to anyone interested in poetry. You can click on Featured Poet and choose a poem by one of the poets you'd like to read. If you click on The Poets Read, you can see and/or hear the poets read their work. In addition, the Lesson Plan link offers a "Style Sheet for Revising Poetry," something that is likely to help the teacher who's just not sure what to say about a student's poem. At the Teaching Strategies link, you can find a helpful section called How and Why They Teach, brief suggestions by teachers.

Finally, "Fooling with Words with Bill Moyers" offers over 80 sites that you can access with a click of the mouse in categories like "Online Poetry," "Publishers and Magazines," and "Off the Beaten Path." These sites are loaded with goodies for the poetry fan. I especially liked some of the publishers' sites, like The Atlantic Monthly and Copper Canyon Press. If you're not familiar with the Teachers and Writers Collaborative, its link in the "Writers' Resources" section is worth investigating.

POETRY DAILY (http://www.poems.com)
If you love the thought of opening your browser every morning and finding a new poem, this is the site for you. Trust me. "Poetry Daily" is an anthology of contemporary poems that are chosen from books, magazines, and journals currently in print. In addition, the site also offers information about the featured poet and news from the poetry world. Published by a not-for-profit corporation, "Poetry Daily" wants to "broaden access to and foster appreciation for contemporary poetry." And they'll deliver a new poem each day from a wide array of poets, both well known and not. Among those to appear are Wendy Barker, Philip Booth, and Billy Collins.

If you'd like to browse—which is what I like to do from time to time, looking for something new—click on the Archives link and you'll find options to search according to the name of the poet or the poem, or the date a poem appeared in Poetry Daily. In addition, feature articles are also archived.

Poetry Daily also offers a weekly e-mail newsletter, which provides poetry-related news items and a list of new poetry books. The newsletter also notes the poets offered on the daily poem during the current week and the previous week, all of which are available for downloading and printing.

POETRY IN MOTION (www.poetrysociety.org/motion)

If you teach in an urban area, this is one site you and your students should investigate. Developed by the Poetry Society of America and the New York City Transit Authority in 1992 to make bus and subway riding "a more pleasurable and enlightening experience," the program places poem-placards in advertising spaces in subway cards and buses. The program is now available in 14 U.S. cities. You can receive three free poetry posters for your classroom by writing to the address on the site.

The site offers two neat features. One is the Poetry Society of America Atlas, a searchable collection of 10 poems from each of 10 cities that have participated in the Poetry in Motion program. Click on Los Angeles, for example, and you will find poems by e. e. cummings and Czeslaw Milosz. An excerpt of Poe's "The Bells" is one of the poems listed in Baltimore. Click on Dallas and you'll find a excerpt from Romeo and Juliet and "En La Sangre" ("In The Blood") by Pat Mora. The other neat feature of this site is the Poetry in Motion Postcards. You have a choice of nine electronic postcards to send, each with one of the poems as it appears on the colorful poetry posters. "Window" by Carl Sandburg and "Hope is the Thing with Feathers" by Emily Dickinson are two of the choices.

As long as you are at this site, you might want to backtrack a bit and take a peek at the Poetry Society of America site. The Resources link contains connections to sites for poetry journals, book publishers, and (always helpful when I travel) independent literary bookstores. The Crossroads link offers a sampling of articles from P.S.A.'s journal. Another link, updated weekly, takes you to Publisher's Weekly reviews of the latest poetry books.

ONLINE POETRY CLASSROOM (www.onlinepoetryclassroom.org)

This site, maintained by The Academy of American Poets, is the most extensive teacher-centered site that I've come across. Not only does this site include a few hundred poems—from Angelou to Yeats—but it gives the reader a chance to search hundreds of links, organized in categories like "What to Teach," "How to Teach," and "Teacher Forums." It offers curriculum units and lesson plans, pedagogical and critical essays, and a database of teaching standards from around the country. The Teacher Resource Center includes links to education technology, sites created by teachers, and listservs.

A more academic site than most of the others I've included, it provides a strong sense of com-

Web Sites for Individual Poets

The web sites that I've included in this section have one thing in common. They all have at least one component that includes poetry to read, download, and print. That was a crucial criterion for selecting sites. However, there are a number of sites developed by individual poets that are worth visiting. Some sites are maintained by publishers. Scholastic's web site for teachers—<http://teacher. scholastic.com/activities/>—contains an "Authors & Books" link, where you can check out Scholastic writers. The Gary Soto page, for example, includes a biography of Soto, a list of the books he's written, a kit if you'd like to arrange a visit, and a link to the author's web site. In addition, Scholastic has added a new Poetry Writing link, with lessons provided by Karla Kuskin and Jack Prelutsky. So, if you are looking for a poet's web site, a way to find one may be through a publisher.

Other poets maintain their own web sites. I'm always partial to poet web sites where you can read poems, or, better yet, hear the poet read her own work. Two of my favorites sites are those of Kristine O'Connell George and Janet S. Wong. At both, you and your students can hear the poets read their poems. George's site <www.kristinegeorge.com> was judged an American Library Association Great Web Site for Kids, and it's easy to see why. It's pretty to look at and easy to navigate. She has a section for teachers and one for students. You can find her poems at the Poetry Aloud! link. Wong's site is quite fetching, with illustrations by Julie Paschkis, who illustrated several of her books. Wong also has a section where the poetry fan can listen to her read her poems.

If you can't find an author link at the publisher's site, do a quick search on a search engine (like Google, Altavista, and Ask Jeeves) to see if the author does, in fact, have a site. Just go to your search engine, type in the author's name, and see what comes up. That's how I found these sites:

Joseph Bruchac	www.josephbruchac.com
Kalli Dakos	www.kallidakos.com
Ralph Fletcher	www.ralphfletcher.com
Mary Ann Hoberman	www.maryannhoberman.com
Patricia Hubbell	www.kidspoet.com
X.J. & Dorothy M. Kennedy	www.xjanddorothymkennedy.com
J. Patrick Lewis	www.jpatricklewis.com
Marilyn Singer	www.marilynsinger.net
Jane Yolen	www.janeyolen.com

munity for those teachers who are looking for ways to teach poetry to young adults. If you're going to investigate this site—and I would recommend that you do, especially if you teach older, more academic students—make sure to give yourself plenty of time because it is loaded.

THE UNITED STATES OF POETRY (www.worldofpoetry.org/usop)

"The United States of Poetry" was a five-part, award-winning PBS series that appeared in 1996. It was a portrait of our country as seen through the eyes and words of its poets. On the site map, the United States is divided into six regions, each with its own theme: The Land and the People, A Day in the Life, The American Dream, Love and Sex, The Word, and Portraits. By clicking on a region, you open the collection of poems with the corresponding theme. For example, "The American Dreams" contains the work of 10 poets, including cowboy poet, Vess Quinlan; Canadian cult rocker, Leonard Cohen; and Beat icon Lawrence Ferlinghetti, all presented with intriguing graphics.

E-VERSE (www.milkweed.org/3_1.html)

Okay, if a poem a day is a bit too much for you, then E-verse might be more to your liking, since it delivers "a new poem—current or classic" to your e-mail box every Monday. This site is maintained by Milkweed Editions, a nonprofit literary press "publishing with the intent of making a humane impact on society" and believing that literature is a "transformative art uniquely able to convey the essential experiences of the human heart and spirit." E-verse offers no archives or other goodies, just an interesting poem every Monday morning. Although its offerings are modest, this site, like Poetry Daily, is an excellent way for you to meet new poets.

Audio Books

Using audio books to teach poetry is often overlooked. With the new compact disc technology, it's easier than ever to bring the poets—or at least their voices—into your classroom. The single best source of information about audio books is a monthly magazine called *AudioFile*. Packed with scores of reviews of audio programs of all sorts on cassettes and CDs, *AudioFile* also offers to subscribers to their print magazine a section of their web site—www.audiofilemagazine.com—that allows you search through more than 10,000 archived reviews for specific types of programs.

The poetry archive site holds reviews of well over 200 audio programs, from *Beowulf, A Child's Garden of Verses,* and *An Anthology of African-American Poetry for Young People* to individual programs by Pablo Neruda, Jack Kerouac, and Michael Rosen. You can easily search this site by title, author, subject, and key word. Once you locate information about a recording, you can pursue it at your local bookstore or library, which, if it's like most libraries, has an ever-expanding array of audio programs.

Although the work of many of the "classic poets"—such as Frost, cummings, Eliot, Plath—are reissues of records, the programs have been electronically cleaned up, and frequently offer illuminating liner notes. Newer programs are, of course, digitally recorded, so the sound quality is quite good. And, be warned, not all poets are good readers of their work. In fact, many of them are disappointing readers. Regardless of the quality of the recording or the performance by a poet, an audio program is a great way to bring the sound of a poet into your classroom. Here are a few programs that might interest you or your students. Try to get hold of one and maybe give it a listen on your morning drive to school. Have you ever started a day listening to Robert Frost or Maya Angelou? It's a gas!

An Anthology of African-American Poetry for Young People read by Arna Bontemps, Smithsonian/Folkways.

Ashley Bryan: Poems and Folktales read by Ashley Bryan, Audio Bookshelf.

The Best-Loved Poems of Jacqueline Kennedy Onassis read by various individuals, including Caroline Kennedy, Claire Bloom, Daniel Davis, Viola Davis, Byron Jennings, Ruben Santiago-Hudson, Jennifer Wiltsie, and B.D. Wong; Hyperion Audiobooks.

The Best of Michael Rosen read by Michael Rosen, RDR Books.

The Best Poems of All Time, Volumes I and II read by various individuals, including Eric Stoltz, Michael Beck, Graeme Malcolm, and Keith Szarabajka; Time Warner AudioBooks.

The Best Poems of All Time, volume II read by various individuals, including Natalie Cole, Cynthia

Nixon, D.B. Sweeney, and Graeme Malcolm; Time Warner AudioBooks.

The Dragons Are Singing Tonight read by Jack Prelutsky, Audio Program, Listening Library.

Great American Poetry: Three Centuries of Classics, poems by Anne Bradstreet, Edward Taylor, and others, read by various individuals, including Julie Harris, Vincent Price, and Ed Begley; Audio Editions.

Langston Hughes Reads read by Langston Hughes, Caedmon Audio. This series also includes other poets reading their work, among them, e. e. cummings, Carl Sandburg, Robert Frost, and Sylvia Plath.

The Voice of the Poet edited by J.D. McClatchy, read by Robert Lowell, Random House AudioBooks. This series also includes individual programs by Anne Sexton, Elizabeth Bishop, Sylvia Plath, James Merrill, and W.H. Auden.

Although *AudioFile* offers the most comprehensive listing of audio poetry programs, you might also check publishers' web sites, where they promote their latest audio releases. Ask your librarian about professional journals that review audio programs. Your librarian can direct you to *School Library Journal, Publisher's Weekly, Booklist,* and the like.

A Few Final Words...

"Everyone is an explorer. How could you possibly live your life looking at a door and not open it?"

—*Robert Ballard, oceanographer*

Students are always surprised when I tell them that when I was their age, I didn't care about poetry. I would've rather taken out the trash for my cranky neighbor who smelled like my attic than read poetry. No wonder. The poems I was assigned to read seemed mysteriously impossible to understand. I didn't "get" them, and, after a while, I didn't bother to read them.

I consider myself lucky, given my staggering lack of interest in most things related to school. Somehow I fell in love with words and became a reader of poetry. It's no exaggeration to say that poetry changed my life. Reading poetry has helped me to see, feel, and think in new ways. Everyone deserves the chance to explore themselves and their lives through poetry. I hope this book has given you the opportunity to open the door of the poem for yourself and for your students. Take that step and explore what lies within.

Bibliography

Barks, Coleman, editor and translator. *The Essential Rumi.* San Francisco: HarperSanFrancisco, 1995.

Broyard, Anatole. "A Narrow Escape from Poetry." *New York Times Book Review,* August 14, 1988.

Dunn, Stephen. "An Interview with Philip Booth." *New England Review/Bread Loaf Quarterly.* 9, no. 2 (Winter 1986): 134.

Francis, Robert. *Pot Shots at Poetry.* Ann Arbor, MI: The University of Michigan Press, 1980.

Heard, Georgia. *For the Good of the Earth and Sun: Teaching Poetry.* Portsmouth, NH: Heinemann, 1989.

Hughes, Ted. *Poetry I.* New York: Doubleday, 1970.

Kennedy, X. J. and Dana Gioia. *An Introduction to Poetry.* New York: Longman, 1998.

Janeczko, Paul B., ed. *Poetspeak: In Their Work, About Their Work.* New York: Bradbury Press, 1983.

Packard, William, ed. *The Draft of Poetry.* New York: Doubleday, 1974.

Peacock, Molly. *How to Read a Poem…And Start a Poetry Circle.* New York: Riverhead Books, 1999.

Rosenblatt, Louise. *Literature as Exploration* (5th edition). New York: The Modern Language Association of America, 1995.

Whited, Stephen. "Close Examination." *Book,* September/October 2001.

Credits